The Revd Dr  t Mellitus College,
London. As w   the author of *New
World, New C*   gside her academic
work, Hannah   on and evangelism
among student   worker with UCCF.
The Archbishop of Canterbury's 2021 Lent Book is her first
devotional study.

Zoom Study beginning Feb 24

February 11, 2021

Hannah
Steele

Living
His Story

Revealing the extraordinary
love of God in ordinary ways

First published in Great Britain in 2020

Society for Promoting Christian Knowledge
36 Causton Street
London SW1P 4ST
www.spck.org.uk

British Library Cataloguing-in-Publication Data
A catalogue record for this book is available from the British Library

ISBN 978–0–281–08517–0
eBook ISBN 978–0–281–08518–7

Typeset by Falcon Oast Graphic Art Ltd
First printed in Great Britain by Ashford Colour Press

eBook by Falcon Oast Graphic Art Ltd

This book is dedicated to all those who have allowed me to share the good news of Jesus Christ with them; to those who have believed and to those who haven't.

The privilege has been mine.

Contents

Foreword

During Lent, we are invited to retreat and reflect, to mirror Jesus' time in the wilderness before the celebrations of Easter. To write a Lent book then about evangelism, about going out into the world and spreading the word of Christ, might seem odd. During this pandemic year, however, when we have all been confined to our homes, unable to meet and mingle, we have seen people come to Christ in new ways, through new mediums and messages. We have seen that God continues to work even when our normal systems are disrupted. We have learnt just how dependent we are on God's grace and hope, rather than relying on our own cleverness.

This year has been one which none of us could have imagined. If we'd been told in 2019 that we'd all be wearing masks and staying at home in 2020, if someone had warned us about the death toll and the totally new way of life we've had to adopt, people would have found it difficult to believe. We find it difficult to understand another reality until we are living in it. The Christian story requires us to step into an unbelievable account – a wild tale of a virgin birth, miracles, healing and resurrection from the dead. It invites us to believe in a totally new world; one where God has stepped in and shown us a new way to live, a whole new framework. It is a big step to take, because it challenges the realities we thought we knew – that we are on our own, that life is finite and even that the dead stay dead.

This is a story where we are invited to be not just a reader, but an active participant. The story of Jesus is not just a dead tale, but one which is ongoing. Not only are we introduced to a Jewish preacher who lived and died two thousand years ago in the Middle East, but we encounter the vibrant, living Christ with whom we have a relationship. What does it mean for each of us to be both a teller and a participant in God's great story, to recount something that happened two thousand years ago but continues to happen every day?

Evangelism – the spreading of the gospel – requires us to tell a story that is both universal and deeply personal. Stories are how we connect, how we say something about being collectively human, how we share experiences and realize that we have shared experiences. Stories are how we make sense of the world around us and our place in it. Stories are how we learn more about our identity and our relationships to others.

To explain the kingdom of God, Jesus told the disciples stories about agriculture, parties and work, everyday things people could relate to, so as to build the bridge between the world as it is and the world God holds for us. As Christians, we are called to relate to people's experiences, to understand their hopes, dreams and interests, and see how it might point towards the kingdom God has prepared for us. As we share our stories, we form relationships. We learn to evangelize with dialogue rather than monologue. We learn to talk about Jesus from a place of vulnerability rather than power.

Perhaps the most fantastic thing about the Christian story is that it calls us to step into a world which is turned on its head. Fear becomes hope, hate turns into love, death is transformed into eternal life. We are pulled out from obscurity, isolation and loneliness into relationship – those who are ostracised, marginalized, shunned and alone become a part of God's story in the world, welcomed and accepted.

Each of us reading this book will have different stories – of who we are, of how we came to Christ and why we believe what we do. I hope that in reading this book you are reminded of how important you and your story are to Jesus and his Church and feel empowered to share the good news in your own way and context.

It is my prayer this Lent that this extended period of wilderness during the coronavirus might give us an opportunity to reach out and understand others in their own wilderness, and to offer them welcome and acceptance in God's family. I pray that God will fill us with the Spirit to give us new ways of telling his wonderful story to new audiences, so that together we might reveal God's love to others as it has been revealed to us.

+ + *Justin Cantuar*
Lambeth Palace, London

Introduction

It is a privilege to be asked to write the Archbishop's Lent book for 2021. I had the honour of meeting Archbishop Justin in the summer of 2018 and spent a fascinating couple of hours discussing evangelism with him and the Revd Chris Russell. Archbishop Justin's enthusiasm and commitment to evangelism both personally and publicly was inspiring and infectious and I am delighted to be writing a book on the subject, which is in no small way influenced by that conversation.

One of the ideas that we discussed in that time was a statement made by William Abraham, a Northern Irish theologian, whose book *The Logic of Evangelism* continues to be one of my favourites:

> Evangelism has never depended on a sunny analysis of the culture it is seeking to Christianise; if that were the case, the West would never have been evangelised in the first place . . . there is no good reason why the evangelist should be intimidated by prophets of doom who argue that the prospects for evangelism are bleak in the extreme.[1]

There are many reasons why evangelism is particularly challenging in the UK in the twenty-first century and such challenges should cause us to pause and reflect. However, as Abraham so powerfully reminds us, evangelism's rationale has never depended upon societal conditions around us but on the 'internal logic of the gospel'. The fact is, Christian witness is rooted in God and the good news of the gospel; it is the manner of it that needs to be flexible and creative in response to the changing context.

When I embarked upon writing this book the UK was in the early stages of COVID-19 and I had little idea of what lay ahead in the weeks and months to come. Abraham's reminder of the internal logic of the gospel was again an anchor prompting me to trust that even in such circumstances disciples of Jesus are to find fresh and imaginative ways of sharing the good news.

For the last five years I have lectured on the subject of evangelism at St Mellitus College in London. I am indebted to the students from all walks of life who have studied there and shared their own experiences of evangelism with me, both good and, on occasion, humorously bad. I am particularly grateful for those who have allowed me to share their stories in this book. Writing during a pandemic certainly presented challenges of its own and I could not have done this without the dedication and support of my family and especially my wonderful husband Gavin whose patience and support never wavers, not least in taking on more than his fair share of home-schooling during the lockdown.

Lent may seem an unusual time to focus on the subject of evangelism. After all, isn't Lent supposed to be about laying aside our activism and taking time to reflect, meditate and abstain in order to draw closer to God? Pope Francis reminds us that Jesus himself is 'the first and greatest evangelizer'. As we spend time drawing close to Christ through prayer and reflection, we cannot help but encounter his heart for those who do not yet know the good news of the gospel. Lent is the perfect time to begin inclining our hearts and prayers towards those in our community and in our world around us who need to hear the good news of God's love. Action and words will follow naturally.

Lent prepares us for the events of Holy Week and the pinnacle of the Passion narrative in the resurrection of Jesus Christ from the dead on that first Easter morning. Mary, who was first to see the empty tomb and encounter Jesus in the garden, races back to the disciples with the simple words 'I have seen the Lord'. The good news that Jesus is alive broke into the disciples' fear and sorrow, bringing hope and transformation. It continues to do so today. Like Mary, we too add our words 'I have seen' to the gospel story. Two thousand years later we continue to pass on this earth-shattering news towards which the period of Lent and the journey of Holy Week lead us: Jesus is alive, love has conquered sin and death, new life is possible for those who follow him. Our task as witnesses today is to find ordinary ways of revealing this extraordinary news to those we encounter in our daily lives. My hope and prayer is that this book will give you a fresh perspective on evangelism and help you become more confident and creative in the task of witnessing, to which every disciple of Jesus is called.

1

The greatest story of all time

Evangelism is rooted in the resurrection

Mary Magdalene went and announced to the disciples, 'I have seen the Lord'; and she told them that he had said these things to her.
(John 20.18)

As a young child I loved my grandma's stories. Whenever she came to stay, I would creep into her room first thing in the morning, climb on to the bed and whisper the words 'tell me a ditty', which was the familiar term we used. My grandma was a wonderful story-teller and she would keep us enthralled for hours with her softly spoken poems and ditties. The ones I loved most were those she told of when my mum was a child and how she and her sister used to get up to some mischief. She would tell the same stories over and over again and I was only too happy to listen. I loved hearing them; not only because of my grandmother's rhetorical skill but because they made me feel safe. Through these stories I felt that I belonged somewhere. As I listened to them I came to understand something of who I was and what it was to be part of my family.

The gospel of Jesus Christ is a story. It is a story about God that can be told and recited, studied and analysed, debated and dis-cussed. Robert McKee is a lecturer in storytelling who has coached many Hollywood screenwriters and he says this about our sense of connection with the idea of stories: 'Our appetite for story is a reflection of the profound human need to grasp the pattern of living, not merely as an intellectual exercise, but within a very per-sonal, emotional experience.'[1] We show this appetite through our obsession with books, films and TV programmes whose storylines enthral and entertain us. We also show this hunger through the stories that we tell of our lives, often using a narrative to describe how our day has been. When we meet someone for the first time we tend to get to know them through recounting experiences we have had rather than presenting a list of facts.

The gospel as story

The gospel of Jesus Christ is a story, but it is quite unlike any other story we will ever encounter. In fact it is not something that we simply hear and understand but a reality in which we live and find our sense of belonging. His story is *the* living story that makes sense of all the other stories in our lives. On the first Easter Sunday morning the women set off for the tomb, taking with them spices that they had prepared for Jesus' dead body. They thought the Jesus story had come to an end. Peering into the tomb these women began to grasp that something in the fundamental structure of the world had changed. The graveclothes meant to hold the decaying body of the battered and bruised Messiah were left empty, rendered redundant and obsolete. Though they did not fully realize this at that moment, they had seen into a world where death was no longer the final frontier, where sin did not get the last word. They glimpsed a new world where resurrection is possible and where death is defeated. To the other disciples this announcement initially sounded unbelievable, so much so that they had to check it out for themselves. Even to those who had walked by Jesus' side for three years, listened to him teach, seen him perform miracles over every form of physical and mental sickness and even over nature itself, this new possibility still seemed a step too far. What these disciples discovered that first Easter morning was that the Jesus story was far from over; in fact it was just beginning.

The gospel is the good news of the risen Jesus. It is the narrative which stands at the centre of human history and upon which the Christian faith is built. This story is not primarily a matter of reading and understanding but of living. The empty tomb is an invitation to us to enter into new life in Christ where death is not the end. Being a disciple of this Jesus, then, is to live in the reality of the empty tomb. The good news of the risen Jesus is the story we are called to pass on to others, but somehow we have not been very good at knowing how to do this.

Evangelism as invitation

We call this passing on of the gospel story 'evangelism', but it's a word that is often misunderstood. I suspect that if you stood up in church one Sunday morning and said 'Who wants to do evangelism next Saturday?' you might not get a huge response. And the problem is often in how we phrase the question. We misrepresent evangelism when we imply it is something that is done to people, either willingly or unwillingly. Evangelism's starting point is our recognition that if the gospel is the story in which we find our identity and purpose, then evangelism has to do with the whole of our lives and the way that we live them. Our primary task is not convincing people our way of thinking is right but rather inviting them to participate within this story of the risen Jesus. The Old Testament scholar Walter Brueggemann describes evangelism as 'an invitation and summons to "switch stories" and therefore to change lives'.[2] Evangelism by this definition becomes an invitation not to a set of beliefs but to a new way of living. It is to encounter the one who has risen from the dead and in whom there is new life and a new purpose. It is to place his story at the centre of our lives. Through his story we find our sense of purpose, meaning and belonging.

Exploring evangelism as an invitation to switch stories, to enter into the new reality of a world where death is defeated and Jesus is alive, means that it might be both harder and easier than we imagined. It is harder because the offer is one of switching stories, not simply adding Jesus on to an already full life. It is to swap one way of looking at the world with another. There is a cost to the exchange. As the events of Holy Week show us, for some the cost is too high. Yet evangelism as invitation is also easier than we thought because it is not dependent upon us to make it happen. It is an invitation into an expansive place where the deepest longings and desires of human life are met in Christ, where all our fears about death and the ultimate end come face to face with the one who is risen from the dead. Offering another person the chance to enter into the Easter story is the greatest gift we can give the world. Evangelism is easier than we had imagined because Jesus has opened up to us the very thing that the world really needs. All we need to do is make that offer available to others.

This means that evangelism is one of the most courageous callings upon our life and it is also the greatest privilege on earth. Evangelism should be the most natural thing in the world for disciples of Jesus and yet we have somehow made it feel unnatural and uncomfortable. How might we reimagine evangelism in a way that feels less daunting and in which the invitation to 'switch stories' feels natural? Before we attempt to do this, let's deal with some of the misconceptions about evangelism that I have frequently encountered.

1 Evangelism is for the experts. One of the greatest misconceptions is that evangelism is only for the experts. We tend to think of evangelism as an extraordinary activity rather than an ordinary one. When we think of evangelism we might have a positive image of someone like J. John, a talented public evangelist, who can stand on a platform and speak engagingly to thousands of people about Jesus. However, we know there's no way we could do that and so we assume evangelism is for the experts and can't be for the likes of us. Alternatively, a more negative image of evangelism might pop into our minds. A few months ago I took the tube train to East London, to one of London's busiest street markets. When I stepped out of the tube there was a man standing by himself with a basket full of Christian tracts at his feet. In his hand he was holding a megaphone through which he was shouting, 'The wages of sin are death.' I smiled at him but noticed that everyone else seemed completely to ignore him, carrying on with their conversations and shopping. It was as if he wasn't there. His message was merely background noise to a busy London market on a sunny day. Such experiences as these leave us assuming that evangelism can't possibly be something we are called to do – either because, as in the first case, we don't have the skills or gifts required, or, in the second case, we couldn't ever imagine ourselves doing something that feels so unnatural and embarrassing. In either scenario we assume evangelism is an extraordinary activity most definitely not for ordinary people like us.

2 Evangelism is morally dubious. One of the activities I invite my students to do in our classes on evangelism is to reflect on their positive and negative experiences of evangelism. It doesn't take long till the examples of disastrous evangelistic encounters come flooding in. The worst examples nearly always have in common an evangelism experienced as something that is 'done to' another person. In such scenarios evangelism has made the person on the receiving end of it feel awkward, uncomfortable or even afraid. I have discovered that if you say the word 'evangelism' repeatedly and quickly it ends up sounding like 'vandalism', which is how many of us feel about the subject. A recent Barna survey conducted among Christian millennials (those born between 1984 and 2000) discovered that this age group was morally conflicted about the concept of evangelism.[3] The majority of those interviewed thought that evangelism was an important part of being a disciple but over half of them felt uncomfortable doing it. It seems there is a disconnect between what we think we 'ought' to be doing and what we feel is right. In our increasingly pluralistic culture, where dozens of religions and worldviews live cheek by jowl, we can feel awkward about the idea of persuading someone to our way of thinking. We are fearful of coming across as bigoted or judgemental. We hear stories in the press of Christians being prosecuted for speaking about their faith in the workplace and it strikes us with fear. We wonder whether what we have to say is really good news to those around us. We are also very aware that evangelism done badly can be manipulative and coercive, and so the old adage 'preach the gospel and if necessary use words' can seem a more appealing course of action. Eventually silence about our faith becomes the norm.

3 *Evangelism is irrelevant.* A third misconception about evangelism is that it is irrelevant to people today. You may have attempted to invite someone to church to find that they were not interested; they didn't even give your invitation the time of day. You may have tried to talk about what you do at church with your friends only to be met by blank faces and an awkward silence. The gulf sometimes seems too huge and what a man in Palestine 2,000 years ago had to say just doesn't figure on the conversational agenda. This gulf can be magnified when we spend all our time busy with church activities and feel we have little to say that connects with people. We don't watch the same TV programmes as them or spend time in the same places as them. We are cooped up in our church bubble and the gap between us and the rest of the world grows by the minute. Over the last 50 years the West has experienced a huge cultural shift that has removed Christianity from the central narrative that governs our societal life. Sociologists write books with cheery titles such as *The Death of Christian Britain* and *The Tide is Running Out*, and *The Guardian* posts front-page articles telling us that the Church of England faces a generational catastrophe as less than 2 per cent of young adults identify with it at all and 7 out of 10 under-24s claim they have no religion whatsoever.[4] Our experience is frequently that people are not interested in the core ideas of the Christian faith. Concepts like sin and salvation seem out of touch with the language of ordinary life. And even when we do get into conversation about our faith we face a barrage of questions about the problem of suffering, science and religion or the church's response to various controversial topics. We might fear we do not know how to answer or worry we might say the wrong thing. Once again silence seems like the safest option. Surely God can find some other way or use someone else?

4 *Evangelism is hard work.* For others, we might believe that evangelism is important and we're honestly trying our best but we just don't feel as if we are getting anywhere. I have been praying for some of my friends for over 20 years now. Why am I not seeing anything happen? For some of us our greatest fear about evangelism is not that it is morally dubious or irrelevant but simply that it doesn't work any more. You try and try to live a life that points to Jesus and you have conversations with people about what you believe, but in terms of results you don't have much to show for it. If someone were to ask you when you last introduced someone to Jesus you wouldn't know what to say. You haven't got anything to show for all your hard work. After a while this can become discouraging and even demoralizing. Was it really this hard for the first disciples? All Peter had to do at Pentecost was stand up and preach a sermon and 3,000 people straight away wanted to follow Jesus. What are we doing wrong that we're not seeing that kind of result today? Evangelism just feels like hard work, with very little success.

Beautiful feet

I am a bit squeamish when it comes to feet. They are not my favourite part of the human body. Maundy Thursday is always a particular challenge and a good spiritual discipline for me when it comes to the foot-washing. Feet often show the wear and tear of the busyness of human life; they bear their hard usage in callouses and dirt, particularly for those living in hot climates. A hot, sweaty and dusty foot does not seem very attractive to me. Yet in Romans Paul declares, 'How beautiful are the feet of those who bring good news!' (Romans 10.15). Paul dares us to imagine that something quite ordinary, hard-worn and unglamorous can be a thing of beauty. He was quoting Isaiah, who was referring to the feet of the messengers who would bring the incredible announcement to Judah that the Babylonian exile was over. Those feet would have been far from beautiful, being dirty and tired from the journey, but Isaiah uses poetic language and calls them 'beautiful' because they were the feet that brought a message of hope and freedom. These ordinary feet would have been running swiftly across the mountain terrain, tired from the journey but with a spring in their step because of the extraordinary news they were bringing. The announcement that followed was one of good news, freedom and salvation. These feet were beautiful because their presence signified that a new chapter in the story was being opened up before them. Paul too uses this idea of the beautiful feet to describe those who bring the good news of the gospel of Jesus. However, beautiful is not a word we readily associate with evangelism.

My conviction is that we need a better way to talk about evangelism; a more beautiful one. We need to reimagine evangelism as something that isn't onerous and irrelevant but imaginative and exciting. We need to recapture something of the beauty of evangelism that has got lost in the fear and the awkwardness. Every time we share the good news of Jesus with someone in word or deed we have beautiful feet. We must be reminded once again of why the good news is really good news for those around us. We need to learn not only to say what Jesus did but to communicate in the way that Jesus did. My hope and prayer is that this book will help us do that. So, where should we start in imagining this beautiful evangelism? Let's begin by meeting our four misconceptions with four truths about the reality of evangelism.

1 Evangelism is for all of us (and not just the experts)

When I am teaching on evangelism one of the first things I get people to do is to list all the characteristics that they associate with the word 'evangelist'. These generally range from positive characteristics such as confident, persuasive, talented at speaking, extroverted and funny to more negative characteristics such as insensitive, forceful and even dishonest. I then get people to list the characteristics of the person who has been most influential in their own journey to faith. The answers to this question are normally quite different, including words such as caring, kind, interested, compassionate, honest, full of integrity, authentic and passionate. The reason so many of us struggle to think of ourselves as being any good at evangelism is because we have an image in our heads (whether positive or negative) of someone who is an evangelist by profession, someone who has an extraordinary calling with extraordinary talents. We forget that evangelism is for ordinary people. The first disciples were run-of-the-mill men and women with ordinary jobs and from ordinary backgrounds. It was their encounter with Jesus that was extraordinary. We need to re-imagine evangelism as something more normal and everyday. It is something that each and every one of us can do, however ordinary or inadequate we might feel. We don't need any particular gifts or special qualifications. It is the good news of God's love that is extraordinary.

The term 'evangelist' is not used a great deal in the New Testament; in fact, it appears only three times. Philip is referred to as an 'evangelist' in Acts 21.8. Timothy is urged by Paul to 'do the work of an evangelist' (2 Timothy 4.5) and Paul lists 'evangelist' as one of the five ministries of the Church in Ephesians 4.11. The four Gospel writers later became known as the four Evangelists, but the term is not used to describe the average follower of Jesus. It was a ministry associated with a particular calling and gift. Instead the word more commonly used in the New Testament is the word 'witness'. In the book of Acts, the word witness crops up 23 times. It is used as a noun to describe those who are followers of Jesus, as in Acts 1.8, 'You will be my witnesses', but it is also used as a verb to describe the act of speaking about who Jesus is and the things he has done (Acts 4.33). Eventually the Greek word for witness, *martus* (plural: *martures*), was used to describe those who had died for their faith and from which we get our word 'martyr' today. The New Testament witnesses were those who saw (that is, witnessed) what Jesus had done, spoke about what they had seen and were prepared to die for it. Witnessing was core to what being a disciple of Jesus was all about. Witnessing was not an optional extra for the Christian disciple. It was not a term reserved for the super spiritual or for the particularly enthusiastic follower of Jesus. To be a disciple is to be made a witness. The task of evangelism, then, is not a separate activity but, rather, is characteristic of every aspect of discipleship. The first disciples knew that witnessing was a way of life not an activity to be turned on and off like a tap. To follow Jesus was to be a witness. The two were synonymous. Being a witness was dangerous, but there was no other way to live once you had encountered the risen Jesus. The theologian Stanley Hauerwas expressed it like this:

The life of Christian witness is, as St Paul has come to know by both hearing and also by doing, the truest and best way to live. To be sure it can be lived differently, as Acts shows us by showing so many different witnesses. But each is a full, profoundly interesting life, the life the particular witness was meant for, and which the witness now lives out as a gift received from Christ to whom he or she bears witness.[5]

It was through witnessing that the kingdom grew. The women at the tomb on that first Easter Sunday were the first witnesses to the new reality that Jesus had risen from the dead. Mary Magdalene's simple words 'I have seen the Lord' (John 20.18) mark the beginning of a new era in which the news that death is not the end, that love has conquered evil, that hope will triumph becomes the refrain of the disciples of Jesus. In this way the news of God's death-defying love was passed from person to person, from place to place. The ordinary as vessels of the extraordinary. In fact, it seemed that the 'ordinary' nature of the disciples was part of what made them such effective witnesses: 'Now when they saw the boldness of Peter and John and realized that they were uneducated and ordinary men, they were amazed and recognized them as companions of Jesus' (Acts 4.13). The witness of these early disciples was never a purely rational presentation of the facts as one might expect from a witness in a court room. Those who had witnessed these extraordinary events were not afraid to put their name to it. Witnessing was personal. It was the story of what God had done through Christ on the cross and through the empty tomb, but it was their story also. 'I have seen' became the hallmark of Christian witness. And this simple witness turned the first-century world upside down.

Witnessing then is the call upon each of our lives and is not just for the experts. There are those who are called to be *an* 'evangelist', who have a particular gift in this area and are often skilled at preaching the good news in public and seeing people come to faith. One of the exciting initiatives I am involved in at the moment is the Archbishop's College of Evangelists, which is seeking to raise up 1,000 evangelists in the Church of England. We need evangelists in the Church today to lead the way, setting an example to follow. We need evangelists to pioneer new and creative and courageous ways of preaching the good news of Jesus. But more importantly, we need every ordinary disciple of Jesus today to know that witnessing is in their DNA. Evangelism is not a specialist activity for the keen or the called, but the privilege of every follower of Jesus.

I wonder who was your 'I have seen' person or people? Who pointed you towards Jesus? Perhaps it was a parent, a teacher, a member of the clergy, a friend or colleague. Thank God for them today and start to ask God who he is putting in your path, to whom you can say those simple words 'I have seen' or 'I have found'. Lent could be a great time to commit to pray for those around you, in your places of work or neighbours on your street. When we utter the words 'I have seen', we play our part as missionary disciples of Jesus who witness to the good news. Witnessing is something we can do regardless of whether we have been a Christian for five weeks or for fifty years. It is simply about living our life following Christ and as we do so passing on the message that Jesus is alive. On the one hand, witnessing is nothing particularly out of the ordinary; it is just talking to people about the most important thing in our lives, and we do that all the time about other important things in our lives. Witnessing can take place at a bus stop with a stranger, over a meal with a closest friend or family member, over the garden fence with a neighbour, online or in person. Witnessing is about our everyday relationships, the places where we travel and the places where we live. However, witnessing is also the most remarkable thing we could ever do because the invitation to encounter Jesus and find your place in the story of the one who has risen from the dead is the greatest gift we could ever offer another human being.

Witnessing is the call upon each of our lives as disciples of Jesus. It has always been this way. Through witness, the extraordinary is revealed through the ordinary. Person to person. Place to place. Witnessing is not just for the experts or those who like standing up in front of large crowds. Witnessing is the task and privilege of anyone who is a disciple of Jesus.

2 Evangelism is always invitational (and therefore not morally suspicious)

Every Christmas my husband and I love to host a Christmas party. We spend time planning and preparing for it. My husband spends time crafting the perfect festive playlist while I search online for this year's innovative culinary take on the mince pie. But all this planning and preparation is obsolete without invitations. If there's no one there to enjoy the music, the food and the sparkly lights, then our preparation is in vain. Evangelism in the New Testament is by nature invitational and this way of looking at it helps us distance it from some of the forms of evangelism that make our blood run cold. Our perception that evangelism is somehow morally dubious is based upon a presumption that evangelism might be something we do to someone against their will. As Rebecca Manley Pippert joked, 'There was part of me that secretly felt evangelism was something you shouldn't do to your dog, let alone your friend.'[6] In our pluralistic culture we are generally not fearful of sharing our experience of something or speaking enthusiastically of things we are passionate about. What we are fearful of, however, is coming across as narrow-minded or bigoted or somehow forcing someone to do something against their will. Witness in the New Testament has more to do with sharing personal experience and speaking enthusiastically than judging and coercion. Evangelism is by nature invitational and therefore can never be forceful. An invitation is freely given and it can be accepted, ignored or rejected. Giving an invitation can never be an act of compulsion; to do so would turn it into a demand rather than a free offer.

Some of the greatest evangelists of the modern age have reminded us of the importance of invitation in evangelism. John Finney's research in the 1990s suggested that the most common way for people to start attending church was through an invitation.[7] Similarly, the evangelist J. John suggests that 77 per cent of new church attenders are there because they were invited by a friend or relative.[8] We may pour resources into publicity and social media campaigns but personal invitation continues to be the most effective way.

Zoe, a family support worker, was on her way to work early one crisp December morning and took her normal commute through Peckham Rye station. As she made her way towards the station she could hear the unusual sound of singing. She was in a rush and didn't want to be late for work but she found herself drawn to the carol singers and stopped for a moment to listen. Rushing for her train, she took one of the flyers being handed out, which were advertising the carol service the following week. Zoe was a casual church attender, the sort who might go at Christmas and possibly Easter but never more than that. The next Sunday Zoe and her husband Paddy turned up to the carol service not expecting it to be any different from their usual experience of singing a few carols as part of their festive celebrations. As the service started, something felt different for Zoe; she was aware of people around her singing from their hearts, singing to someone. This wasn't what she expected from her annual carol service. She and her husband came again to church on Christmas Day and again on the first Sunday after Christmas. In that service Zoe found herself in floods of tears and she didn't know why. All she knew was that she had to come back again the next week.

During the next few weeks Zoe and Paddy became part of the community that Zoe had first heard singing that frosty December morning. In time she came to see that her emotional response was the Spirit at work within her. They both realized that the singing from the heart that so moved them at that carol service was because those singing were captivated not merely by an ancient story of a baby in a manger but by Jesus whom they could encounter now. In different ways both Zoe and Paddy came to know this Jesus for themselves and this relationship with him has given them a new sense of purpose with God at the centre of their lives. That December morning Zoe wasn't particularly aware of her need for God in her life. On the outside it looked as though she had the ideal life: a lovely family, a nice house and a job she found fulfilling. Looking back, Zoe sees that there was a faith-shaped hole in her life that she was simply unaware of.

Each day thousands of people travel through Peckham Rye

station on their way to work and school and home. But on one of those 365 days a small group of people chose to get up even earlier, sing some carols and hand out some invitations. Many of those invitations will have been placed in a pocket and forgotten about. Others are immediately discarded and swept up with the coffee cups and litter left along the way. But one invitation made all the difference. One invitation became an invitation not only to church but to an encounter with Jesus which turned a whole family's life around.

Because evangelism is invitational by nature we need to ensure that we think creatively and courageously about how we invite people to church. Initiatives such as 'Try Church' or 'Back to Church Sunday' can be really effective in having a specific Sunday on which people are encouraged to invite friends to church and when consideration is given to how the service might be particularly accessible or engaging for those attending for the first time. However, in the New Testament the emphasis in evangelism is not on invitation to church but first and foremost an invitation to Jesus. There can be a danger in assuming that the only invitation that really matters is the one to church because when people refuse that (and many will!) we must not assume that means they have no interest in faith. For many, church is a step too far down the line and they simply are not ready. Evangelism is first and foremost an invitation to come and see who Jesus is, an invitation to move just a step closer, an invitation to begin to peer into the empty tomb as those women did early that Easter morning. Eventually evangelism is an invitation to repent and believe in Jesus but its starting point might be simply to become curious about Jesus.

Come and see

Time and time again in the Gospels we see ordinary people drawn to Jesus. Unlikely people like tax collectors and beggars by the roadside find themselves irresistibly pulled towards him. They find themselves welcomed and loved when others had rejected them. Evangelism is an invitation to see the Jesus who loves the sinner and the broken and who welcomes all. This kind of invitation can happen anywhere – on a bus or a plane, by the water fountain at work, outside the school gates, by the bedside of a sick friend or to the child on your knee during a bedtime story. And it can happen in so many different ways: through acts of love, through the creative arts, through sharing our experience with others, through pointing to the hidden echoes of the story of Jesus in our world today, through prayer and through healing. And accompanying all these things come those oft-said words in the New Testament, 'Come and see'. The Samaritan woman tells her friends to 'Come and see a man who told me everything I have ever done!' (John 4.29). Philip tells Nathanael to 'come and see'. Jesus tells the fishermen to 'come and follow' him.

Evangelism is an invitation not primarily to an event but to an act of imagination, a wondering what life might be like if there was someone who loved us unconditionally. What, even, if that one who loved us unconditionally was risen from the dead? In many of my conversations with so-called 'secular' people this is a refrain I come back to again and again. 'What would it mean if death was not the end?' 'What would it mean if one person had defeated death and been raised to life?' In the beginning of such imaginings beautiful evangelism starts to take its place.

Evangelism is an invitation to see life in a different way. And because it is an invitation it is offered and not coerced. Evangelism that is manipulative or forced beyond what someone is comfortable with ceases to be like an invitation and ends up being more like a conscription. God, the great invitation-giver, does not hunt down those who decline it and demand a reason. The invitation is offered freely and generously, without a hidden agenda or catch. Our role as witnesses to this good news is to be bold and creative in invitation but never forceful or demanding.

3 Evangelism is responsive (and therefore not irrelevant)

The word evangelism originates in the Greek word *evangel*, which means good news. Mark Russell is the CEO of the Children's Society and he describes evangelism in the following way:

Evangelism is above all about good news! It is the good news that God loves us, that God sent Jesus. It's good news that brings hope to the poor, freedom for the prisoner, recovery of the sight for the blind. It's good news that releases the oppressed and proclaims the year of the Lord's favour. We have an amazing story to tell, a story of Jesus, a story of love, a story that transforms lives.[9]

At the centre of the Christian faith is something that is very good news. Jesus uses the image of buried treasure to describe what this good news is like (Matthew 13.44). The treasure is hidden away but when someone finds it they are so excited that they sell everything they own in order to buy the field and possess the fortune. The treasure that is found is of such immense value that it is worth giving up everything for. The gospel is by nature good news in and of itself. The 'goodness' of the message is not dependent upon our reception of it, yet it only becomes good news to us when we are willing to receive it.

One of the remarkable things about the Christian gospel is that it is both wonderfully complex and beautifully simple. I work in a theological college and so am surrounded by people who are spending their lives exploring the complexities of the gospel. We could spend a lifetime exploring the Scriptures and never exhaust the depths of what it means that Jesus is good news for us. During Lent we spend 40 days preparing our hearts for the events of Holy Week and Easter because they are of such great significance to us. However, the good news of Jesus is also so beautifully simple that a child can understand it and respond. While there are a myriad things we can say about the nature of the gospel, let's simply look at three things the gospel tells us which mean it is a message of good news for all people in any time or place. The gospel is good news for us because it addresses our deepest needs and longings as human beings.

(a) The gospel tells us we are loved
In a recent trip to the USA my American friends were excited to take me to the In-N-Out Burger bar, which they assured me I would

19

love. Quite unlike any burger restaurant I have visited in the UK, In-N-Out is a Christian franchise, famous for secret Bible verses hidden on its packaging. It's a form of evangelism by stealth, I suppose. I was intrigued to see the words 'John 3.16' written on the bottom of my empty drinks cup. My friends were right, I did enjoy the experience although I wondered whether the average person going out for a burger would bother to look at the base of their drinks cup and, if they did, would they have a clue what John 3.16 meant? (This, by the way, was the most famous verse printed; the chip packets and burger packs had verses I certainly did not know by heart.) Thankfully, however, the true message of the gospel is not hidden away in obscure packaging but declares loud and clear that we are loved extravagantly and abundantly. The gospel deals with our deepest need to be known, loved and accepted.

The high street jewellery shop Pandora's Valentine's Day campaign in 2020 was 'Show her that you know her'. I did a double take when I saw this for the first time at London Bridge station. Surely the line is 'Show her that you love her'? But perhaps to be known is to be loved. It is often the case that presents that are chosen with true knowledge of us are better gifts than the more extravagant or expensive ones. In a world where we are increasingly anonymous, a swipe on a credit card, self-checking out our weekly shop, a pre-ordered drink without even having to eyeball the barista, discovering that someone truly knows us is powerful indeed. Is it the case that the most meaningful token of love is one that shows we have been seen and that tells us we are known?

When Hagar, Abraham's maidservant who is treated badly by him and his wife, flees to the desert, ashamed and abandoned by the one she thought was her provider, God reveals himself to her as the God who sees (Genesis 16.13). Hiding away in shame and dishonour, Hagar is reassured by the God of the universe that she is seen and therefore known. This declaration of being seen and noticed by God becomes the foundation from which she is able to return to Abraham and rebuild her life.

Gail Honeyman's book *Eleanor Oliphant is Completely Fine* tells the heart-warming and gut-wrenching tale of a woman who feels she does not fit.[10] Through this woman's story our society's lone-liness is narrated and laid bare before our eyes. It is a fictional retelling of the fact that for many people in our society today isolation is inevitable. Age UK suggests that 1.4 million older people are chronically lonely. The current global pandemic has only served to demonstrate the loneliness epidemic that has been present for far longer.

The gospel of Jesus Christ tells us that we are seen, known and loved. I love that it is Mary who is first to greet Jesus after his resurrection. It is to a woman, previously shunned and ashamed, now seen face to face, that Jesus utters the simple word 'Mary'. In that moment she is seen and known and it becomes the foundation upon which she becomes the first witness to the resurrection of Christ. The gospel of Jesus is good news because it tells us that we are seen, known and loved with an extraordinary love.

(b) The gospel tells us we are forgiven

The second reason that the gospel is good news for our world today is because it tells us that we are forgiven. The gospel deals with our biggest problem as human beings: sin. As Paul writes, 'All have sinned and fall short of the glory of God' (Romans 3.23). There is not one person to whom this statement does not apply. However, we do not find it easy to talk about sin with our friends. It feels an outdated concept in a world of self-fulfilment and personal discovery. As autonomous secular individuals the idea of there being a God we have somehow wronged feels archaic. However, the awareness of our own fallibility and our propensity to harm those around us has not disappeared. I remember talking with a friend of mine about her nephew who had come to her in distress, wracked with guilt at some of the selfish choices he had made in life and the consequences he was now having to face. My friend is not a Christian and she said that she struggled to know what to say to him other than that he had indeed made poor decisions for which he was now paying the price. However, she desperately wanted to know how to deal with the sense of shame and guilt he felt, but didn't know what to say. When we take God out of the picture we are left utterly powerless in the face of our own brokenness, unable to fix ourselves or put everything right.

This is one of the ways in which we need to imagine a better way of talking to people about the gospel. Scripture talks about sin in a variety of ways; our role as witnesses is to choose the most appropriate way to talk about it to the person sitting before us. One of the most common ways Christians talk about sin is in terms of 'breaking the law'. However, this approach really does not engage with postmodern people who are on the whole relativists and will follow up the suggestion that sin is breaking God's moral standards with the comment, 'Who says those standards are right?' We soon find that the conversation ends up being a defence of the idea of truth against the relativistic notion that all perspectives are equally valid, and we are suddenly heading down a rabbit warren we did not intend.

An alternative way that Scripture talks about sin, which perhaps resonates more with people today, is the idea of sin as idolatry. To make an idol out of something is to assign all your love and devotion to it rather than to the God who made you and loves you. We are surrounded by the consequences of pursuing other things before God, whether that is in terms of addiction or broken relationships. If people are able to see the consequences of 'sin' as harmful for the flourishing of human life then they are more likely to be receptive to the good news that God offers a way of freedom in Christ from such devotions which can ultimately ensnare and even destroy us.

Others will not struggle with the idea of sin because they already feel worthless or full of shame, possibly even for things done to them. For people such as this, the gospel message is one of freedom from shame, and acceptance and love. While the gospel makes clear our human sinfulness, it makes even more abundantly clear Jesus' relentless and extravagant love for us. For those who feel false shame or unworthiness, our conversations must always fall on the side of radical love and acceptance, just as Jesus' did.

We must also consider our own attitude when talking about sin. Many evangelistic attempts are damaged by Christians who give the impression that sin is what non-believers do. The least appealing characteristic in someone seeking to share their faith is judgementalism. Our role as witnesses is not to convince people that they are sinners. That's the work of the Holy Spirit, not ours to engineer. Yet the gospel of Jesus declares that we are all indeed sinners, that we have a problem we cannot talk our way out of or fix by ourselves. Witnesses to the gospel then speak not from a place of moral superiority but from their own experience of brokenness and shame. All sin has a cost and the cost is paid by Christ on the cross. As the Apostle Peter writes, 'For Christ also suffered for sins once for all, the righteous for the unrighteous, in order to bring you to God' (1 Peter 3.18).

The good news of the gospel is that Jesus, the righteous one who lived a perfect life, has taken our place on the cross. The events of Good Friday announce to us that while we may be more sinful than we even realize, we are loved more than we could dare to hope or imagine. One of the things that Jesus was criticized for by the religious leaders of the day was his choice of dinner guests and friends. His decision to dine with the less respectable characters caused quite a stir. In responding to these criticisms, Jesus replied, 'Those who are well have no need of a physician, but those who are sick; I have come to call not the righteous but sinners' (Mark 2.17). The good news of the gospel is that Jesus has come for sinners like you and me. Forgiveness is the greatest gift that transforms our life, our relationships and ultimately our relationship with God. Like the prodigal son, we too are welcomed home. There is no greater privilege than sharing this good news of forgiveness with those around us.

(c) The gospel tells us we do not have to fear death

It has been significant to be writing this book during a global pandemic and in particular reflecting on the good news of Jesus in the face of our deepest fears. The pandemic has forced us to come face to face with our own mortality in a way this generation has not previously experienced. During the first week of lockdown the fear was tangible; within a matter of hours we suddenly found ourselves locked inside our homes, afraid to go out and watching the death toll slowly mount, with the tragic losses of key workers who had very literally put their lives on the line in the face of this ruthless virus. A feeling of powerlessness seemed to pervade friends and family, and many of us have lost loved ones or know people close to us for whom this has been a devastating experience. COVID-19 compelled us to recognize our own powerlessness in the face of our mortality in a way that is normally hidden much deeper below the surface. Despite our attempts to control the helplessness we felt by stockpiling pasta and toilet paper, our mortality could not be hidden.

One of the most remarkable stories in the Gospels is of Jesus' visits to Mary and Martha after the death of their brother Lazarus. Martha sometimes gets a bad press in comparison with her sister Mary, but I love the brazen honesty of her response to Jesus for turning up so late: 'Lord, if you had been here, my brother would not have died' (John 11.21). Faced with this tragic situation, John tells us that Jesus stood by the grave and wept. There is nothing natural about death; it is a rupture in the very fabric of our human existence. Despite the many philosophies and worldviews that influence our culture today and suggest that death is the natural end to human life, Scripture refers to death as the final enemy (1 Corinthians 15.24–26) and a strategy of the enemy to make us live in fear (Hebrews 2.15). For many in our culture, the tragedy of this last year has made us confront the fear of death in a brutal way. Death flies in the face of our pursuit of meaning and eternal significance. As Dr Strange says in the Marvel film bearing his name, 'Time is what enslaves us. Death is an insult, we are all looking for the eternal.'[11] In raising Lazarus from the dead, Jesus demonstrated power in the face of the final enemy, an event that prefigured his own resurrection on Easter Sunday some months later.

Witness is built on the foundation of the resurrection. As we have seen, the primary words to leave the mouth of the first ever witness were, 'I have seen the Lord.' To bear witness to the good news is to proclaim loud and clear that Jesus is alive, that death has been defeated and that our deepest fear has been met with resurrection and new life. Christian witness therefore stands or falls on an event of history. The gospel is good news about an event that actually happened; it is not merely a record of spiritual teaching or rules for life. To announce that the final enemy has been defeated and that there is one who has risen from the grave is not a matter purely for personal piety but is of public importance. As Willie Jennings writes:

> To speak of the resurrection of Jesus is no longer religious speech, but speech that challenges reality, reorients how we see earth and sky, water and dirt, land and animals, and even our own bodies. This is speech that evokes a decision; either laugh at it or listen to it, either leave or draw near to this body.[12]

The resurrection of Jesus is of such earth-shattering consequence that it can't possibly be irrelevant. Just as the gospel's declaration that we are loved and forgiven speaks into the heart of human existence, so the promise of new life in the name of Jesus cannot possibly be hidden or kept out of sight.

The relevance of the gospel

So what do we make, then, of our perception that evangelism is irrelevant and out of touch? It cannot be that the gospel itself is out of date. However, it is sadly so often our own presentation of it that fails to connect with the reality of people's ordinary lives. Words like 'sin' and 'salvation' fail to connect with people and we all too easily assume that it must be the gospel that is out of touch. What we need is not a new gospel but a more beautiful and imaginative way of speaking of it and connecting with those around us.

This is what it means to be a witness. As witnesses, one of our roles is to connect this story with the stories of those that we meet. Our job is not to change the story to try and make it fit better with contemporary values. Our role is to help people to see its relevance and significance to them. We do this in a number of ways, through speaking of our own story and talking of the difference that Jesus makes here and now. We do it through connecting the gospel with the stories that shape our cultural landscape, which so often point to the gospel but which we can often fail to see. We do it through listening to others and finding points of connection. We do it through prayer and through living out the story in our character and actions.

What is needed is not a new gospel but a new way of imagining witness and evangelism so we might become more effective at making the connection points with those we meet. It is a task for the imagination. Pascal famously said that 'we must make good people wish that the Christian faith were true and then show that it is'. For too long we have been preoccupied with trying to convince people that the Christian faith is true rather than making them wish that it were. Imaginative evangelism seeks to create a desire for a gospel that could tell us we are loved and forgiven and have nothing to fear in the face of death. If we were able to create that kind of desire in the conversations we have, then the question of the relevance of the gospel would no longer be an issue.

4 Evangelism is partnership (and therefore we are not on our own)

One of the reasons we can easily get discouraged in evangelism is because we don't always see the results we long to see. For those of us who like instant results and aren't very patient, evangelism in our current post-Christendom climate can be particularly challenging. One of the biggest changes over the last 50 years has been how the Christian narrative has slowly slipped from our corporate memory. As we prepare to celebrate the events of Holy Week and Easter we discover it is a story that is less and less familiar to those around us. Lesslie Newbigin describes it like this: 'A society which has lost its memory is like a ship which has lost its rudder.'[13]

The reality of this cultural shift was brought home to me when my eldest son was at nursery school. It was the Christmas celebration the next day and we were encouraged to send our child dressed as one of the characters from the Christmas story so that they could take part in a nativity play. I did what any mother would do with 24 hours' notice and flung a tea towel on his head, tied it round with a piece of string and found a toy sheep to carry under his arm. As he took his place the next morning on the emerging tableau alongside other hastily dressed tea towel-headed kids, I noticed a few peculiarities. Lurking in the background was a boy dressed as a cowboy and alongside him a young girl dressed up as a witch. All were merrily singing 'Jingle bells' at the tops of their voices. This rather strange-looking nativity scene was both slightly surprising but also completely normal in a world where the Christian faith is no longer being passed on from generation to generation. Purchasing a small crucifix in a jeweller's one day, my aunt was asked whether she 'wanted one with the little man on it or not'.

On the one hand this presents those of us who would take up the mantle of witnesses with an exciting possibility. Just as those first women were able to tell the earth-shattering news of Jesus' resurrection to people who had never heard it before, this is increasingly becoming our reality as well. Many with whom we share this story have no background knowledge to rely on and it means they can hear it fresh. This is certainly the experience my teenage sons have in talking about their faith with their friends. They say many of them have never met a Christian before and so don't really know what one is. This presents us with a huge opportunity to share something exciting and life-changing as if for the first time. But it also presents us with challenges: the journey to faith is often longer for people because the gospel is so far removed from their current experience. Evangelism can feel especially hard if we are relying on methods that are out of date or fail to connect with people. However, as witnesses our role is often no more than nudging people along the pathway, never coercing but gently enabling, sowing seeds of imagination and curiosity about whether this good news could be real after all. My hope and prayer is that this book will provide some ways in which you might start to engage in imaginative evangelism with greater confidence and creativity.

Nevertheless, we can't pretend that evangelism in this current climate is going to be particularly easy. It can be hard work and calls for perseverance and faithfulness. However, it is not something we should be despondent about because we are never alone as witnesses of Jesus. Evangelism is always done in partnership with others and most importantly in partnership with God. This is the great tension that lies at the heart of evangelism, which is both compelling as we discern the importance of playing our part, but also hugely liberating when we realize the results do not depend upon us and we work in partnership with God. How this partnership works and what it means for us will be the subject of our next chapter.

For discussion

1 Can you identify some of the fears or concerns that hold you back from evangelism?
2 In what ways is the good news of Jesus relevant to people in your local community?
3 What are the main characteristics of those who helped you on your journey to faith?

2

Catching up with God

Responding to God's initiative in evangelism

Just so, I tell you, there will be more joy in heaven over one
sinner who repents than over ninety-nine righteous persons
who need no repentance.
(Luke 15.7)

I wonder if you have ever had the experience of God getting there
before you?

Some time ago I was at the hairdresser's on a day off. I had been
working hard all week and all I wanted to do was switch off and
read my book. As I sat in the chair trying to focus on the story
I was reading, the woman cutting my hair started to talk to me.
'Do you work?' she asked. 'Yes,' I replied politely, keeping my eyes
fixed on my book. 'What do you do?' she asked. 'I lecture in theology,' I replied. She paused for a moment and then leant forward
and whispered, 'What's theology?' 'Well,' I replied, 'it's the study of
God.' She looked quizzically at me and said, 'Are you a Christian?' I
nodded and without missing a beat she said, 'Can I ask you a question then? How did you become a Christian, and why?'

At this point I closed my book, placed it down on the counter and
started to share my story with her, talking about my childhood faith
but also my present experience of Christ now as an adult. She listened intently throughout. Midway through my story she stopped
cutting my hair and walked across to the other side of the salon to
collect something. I naturally stopped talking but she called 'Carry
on!' and so I slightly raised my voice and carried on sharing my
testimony. At this point I was aware of the two women either side
of me staring strangely at me. I simply smiled and carried on telling

my story. As my story drew to a close, my hairdresser looked at me intently in the mirror and said the following, 'You know, it's really weird because yesterday I went to church for the first time in 20 years to my friend's son's christening. When I walked into the church I felt something really strange. I had goosebumps all over.' She then rolled up the sleeve of her shirt and said, 'Look! The same thing is happening to me now as you are talking to me.'

This lovely woman had encountered something as she went into church the day before, but she couldn't easily make sense of what was happening to her. As I spoke with her I had the sense I was playing catch-up to what God was already doing. I hadn't particularly sought out this conversation (I had been trying to read my book after all!) but God was clearly at work. All I had to do was to try and help her make sense of what God was already doing in her life and point her towards Jesus. I was aware that she was being drawn towards God; my job was to help nudge her a step further along the path.

This experience, like many I have had, has made me aware that witnessing is not a solitary task. Witnessing is always done in response to God's initiative and in partnership with the Spirit. In my own journey as a witness these two principles of responding to God's initiative and trusting the Spirit's work have transformed the way I view encounters with people. These two principles are so significant in the way we view witnessing that we see Jesus talking about them many times in the Gospels. However, as always, Jesus teaches in unusual, startling and fresh ways and they deserve a further look.

Jesus the storyteller

The Synoptic Gospels (Matthew, Mark and Luke) record Jesus telling over 35 different stories. Over a third of all the recorded words we have by Jesus in the Gospels are parables. Some of these stories are from nature, involving trees, fruit and animals. Others are from the home, telling stories of parents and children, loss and reunion. Others still are from public occasions: banquets and officials, weddings and judges. The sheer breadth of situations and contexts that Jesus used demonstrates his mastery as one of the greatest storytellers who has ever lived. It is remarkable that in our increasingly post-Christian world, which no longer places the Christian faith at the centre of life, some of Jesus' stories continue to remain part of our cultural heritage. Though many are no longer familiar with the stories of Scripture, the phrases 'the good Samaritan' and 'the prodigal son' are still commonly used.

The Sunday school definition of parables that I was taught as a child was that they were 'an earthly story with a heavenly meaning'. I am not convinced that this is what they are. This definition makes them sound like honourable tales with a moral point, on a par with Aesop's fables. Jesus does not use parables to explain abstract theology in concrete terms; instead, his parables demonstrate the revolutionary nature of the kingdom he was announcing. The word *parabolē* in Greek suggests 'putting things side by side ... a putting together of ideas from different spheres in such a way that the one idea illuminates the other'.[1] Jesus' parables illuminated the reality of the new kingdom he was ushering in; they sought to challenge and subvert the normal understanding of how things are or should be. They sought to offer an entirely different way of seeing the world; the topsy-turvy world of the kingdom of God.

Since Jesus' parables so often speak of the kingdom of God, they are therefore pertinent as we seek to get our heads around this somewhat peculiar word 'evangelism'. If evangelism is first and foremost an invitation to enter into God's story then the parables can help us picture what it means to enter into and receive this new kingdom. Parables can provide us with a precious window into this alternative way of being in the world, revealing the extraordinary through the ordinary. In particular we will explore how these two principles that I encountered at the hairdresser's are seen through Jesus' parables. These two lessons can help us become more confident as we seek to invite others into this new way of life in the kingdom.

1 Respond to God's initiative of love

The first thing that Jesus' parables reveal to us is that God takes the initiative in evangelism because God loves people who are lost.

Sam Mendes' epic one-shot movie *1917* tells the story of an against-all-odds race against time during the First World War. Two young soldiers are commissioned with the seemingly impossible task of delivering an urgent message across enemy borders, with the hope of saving the lives of 1,600 soldiers. In one scene, as Lance Corporal Schofield struggles to make his way through the muddy and crammed trenches as gunshots fire overhead, he climbs out of the trenches, running horizontally across the ridge of the trench, dodging gunfire, leaping over bodies, colliding with soldiers clambering over the top and repeatedly picking himself up again and again. It is one of the iconic shots of the film: a desperate man with a lifesaving message prepared to lose his life in the pursuit of its delivery.

The origin of the word evangelism in the New Testament similarly has this sense of an urgent message brought in a critical time in the life of a nation. The word *euangelion*, meaning *Gospel*, is used by Jesus to describe the new way of living that he is ushering in. In fact, Mark places as the very first words on the lips of Jesus, 'The time is fulfilled, and the kingdom of God has come near; repent, and believe in the good news' (Mark 1.15). Mark wanted his readers to know who Jesus is and that what he has come to do is all about the good news of the gospel. Paul too summarizes his message about Jesus as 'the gospel of God . . . concerning his Son' (Romans 1.1, 3).

In the Graeco-Roman world, *euangelion* signified 'the reward' given to a messenger for bringing an announcement, which was usually good news and pronounced a forthcoming time of victory or at least relief for its listeners. In time, the term came to be used for the message itself, but carries with it this sense of a message with an associated reward. It is also connected with the Hebrew verb *bisser*, meaning to announce or deliver a message (whether good or bad). In 1 Kings 1.42 and Jeremiah 20.15, it is used in connection with declaring the appointment of a king and then the birth of a child. In Psalm 40.9 and 10 and Isaiah 41.27, *bisser* is used to proclaim God's victory over the world and his kingly rule. It is the announcement of a new era of God's rule and reign. This announcement of good news (gospel) has both present and future connotations: a new era is on the way but it is inaugurated now. In this way, Jesus' announcement in Luke 4, as he reads from the scroll, that he has been anointed to 'bring good news to the poor' (Luke 4.18) declares that this much anticipated time of 'good news' begins now. Evangelism, then, is the proclaiming of this good news of Jesus in a way that is urgent, compelling and invitational.

An urgent message

Jesus himself told a story about an urgent and compelling invitation. In Luke 14.15–24 we read the story of a man who prepares a lavish banquet. But on the day when his guests are supposed to arrive, one by one they make their excuses not to attend. Angered by this response, the master instead commands his servant to go into the town and bring in anyone he can find, including those who are not normally invited to such prestigious gatherings. Parables such as these would have been shocking to Jesus' listeners, particularly the religious who considered themselves safely on the list of those invited. Through these parables, Jesus asks who are the recipients of this good news and suggests that it is not the prestigious and important people, those who simply assume they are invited. Jesus' extraordinary kingdom prioritized the poor, the neglected, those who didn't think they stood a chance.

The parable of the banquet, like those of the lost sheep, the lost coin and the lost son in the following chapter of Luke, reveal God's heart for those who are not yet part of his kingdom. Central to the notion of evangelism is this simple yet profound theological truth: God loves. Any understanding of evangelism that takes its starting point from anywhere else can so easily become coercive, manipulative or purely pragmatic. The overarching narrative of Scripture is that God loves people. Evangelism, then, finds its ultimate motivation not in the crisis of a church in decline that needs to act in order to prevent its own extinction. Evangelism is always only and ever because God is love. Our witnessing, therefore, is only ever in response to the invitation that God has already made. As I discovered that day at the hairdresser, my role as a witness was to follow up and speak clearly of the invitation God was already making.

Missio Dei

In theological terms, this conviction is often expressed as *missio Dei*, a Latin phrase meaning 'the mission or sending of God'. This concept was articulated at a conference on mission in 1932 by the theologian Karl Barth. This signified a move away from understanding mission as something that the church *did* in response to God's action, and instead reimagined mission as rooted primarily in God's being and his intention in the world. The term *missio Dei* was later formed and identifies God himself as the initiator of mission rather than the Church or any other Christian organization. While mission is far broader than evangelism and encompasses the scope of the Church's presence and action in the world, such as social justice and environmental concern, the call upon the Church to witness is an integral part of its mission. Understanding mission as primarily rooted in the nature and purpose of God means also that evangelism is not our clever idea or a calculated response to try and boost church membership during a period of decline. Evangelism finds its rationale and origin in the love of God for the world, and this theme bubbles over in many of Jesus' parables.

The three lost things (a sheep, a coin and a son) collectively focus on the one who is seeking. In turn, the shepherd, the woman and the father seek diligently and sacrificially for the one that is lost. First, the shepherd leaves behind the 99 that are safe (by all accounts a high-risk strategy) and looks for the one that is lost. The woman, though she has nine other coins, is not prepared to wait for the natural light of morning but uses valuable resources to search thoroughly until the one missing is found. Finally, the father, whose son has severed his familial ties and set off for an independent life, glimpses his son in the distance and runs towards him, silencing the prodigal's cries of regret and remorse with joyful celebration.

In these stories Jesus teaches the religious leaders, who chastise him (as they do on several occasions) for his questionable choice of dinner guests, that God's love is for the lost, the least and even the lawbreaker. In so doing, he challenges them that they should not be surprised that the Messiah acts in this way. God's love is and has always been for such as these.

Christ Jesus came into the world to save sinners

Reading the Bible as the story of God's love

God's missional heart is revealed throughout the scriptural narrative. Chris Wright suggests that exploring the story of the Bible in this way is to approach it with a 'missional hermeneutic', a way of reading Scripture as telling us the story of God who is a missionary and intervenes through human history to bring about his purposes of salvation. And if you read the conversation between the risen Jesus and his disciples at the end of Luke's Gospel, it appears that he approaches Scripture in this way:

> Then he opened their minds to understand the scriptures, and he said to them, 'Thus it is written, that the Messiah is to suffer and to rise from the dead on the third day, and that repentance and forgiveness of sins is to be proclaimed in his name to all nations.'
> (Luke 24.45–47)

In this way Jesus acknowledges that the Scriptures tell the story of a missionary God whose desire is that 'all nations' receive forgiveness for sin. This narrative reaches its fulfilment in the person of Christ, his death and his resurrection. In this conversation Jesus is showing that the story of the Bible is all pointing towards this new way of life in the kingdom of God into which we are invited. Scripture is his story. Evangelism is the invitation to enter into the new life in Christ to which Scripture points.

Evangelism, then, has a Trinitarian basis and is *theocentric* (finding its origin in God) rather than *anthropocentric* (finding its origin in the needs of humanity). Evangelism is defined, directed, energized and accomplished by God. God's love lies at the heart of the invitation to new life in the kingdom of God.

The biblical story reveals God as love. Before the creation of the world God exists as a triune community of love. There is a mutual giving and receiving of love between God the Father, the Son and the Spirit. That is how John can claim in 1 John 4.8 that 'God is love'. God didn't just start loving when he created human beings whom he could love. Humanity does not fulfil any need within God to express or receive love. He is love in himself, in his very nature. Repeatedly Scripture records the compassion and love of God as a Father showing compassion to his children (Psalm 103.13). Even God's anger at the repeated disobedience of Israel stirs his heart of compassion for them (Hosea 11.8). From Genesis to Revelation God intervenes in the story of human history through acts of love, which are expressed ultimately through his sending of his only son, Jesus (John 3.16).

Jesus' choice of dinner guests, therefore, should not have surprised the Jewish religious leaders (Luke 15.2) who prided themselves on their knowledge of Scripture, since, from the beginning of the Old Testament, God is revealed as having concern and compassion for people; his benevolence and mercy are revealed in his election of the people of Israel and his missionary heart is apparent in the calling given to Abraham:

'Go from your country and your kindred and your father's house to the land that I will show you. I will make of you a great nation, and I will bless you, and make your name great, so that you will be a blessing. I will bless those who bless you, and the one who curses you I will curse; and in you all the families of the earth shall be blessed.'
(Genesis 12.1–3)

Abraham is called to leave the security of his home in order to be part of God's fulfilment of his purposes for the world. Abraham is promised a land and is assured that his descendants will be great, plentiful and blessed by God. However, this election does not concern Abraham and his offspring alone; through this nation God will bless the whole earth. Election and covenant, therefore, are not exclusive terms but missional ones. God's concern is not just for the people of Israel but for the whole world, and his people are to reflect that concern. This outward orientation of the people of God was to serve as a sign for all to see. They were to be a display people, pointing to the God of all creation.

God's concern for the non-Jew is seen throughout the Old Testament. Ruth, a Moabite woman, is included in the people of

God and is even grandmother to King David. Rahab, a Gentile prostitute, is listed in Hebrews 11 as being a woman of faith. Through the prophets God rebukes his people for failing to understand that their election was about service and for failing to show compassion to the stranger in their midst (Zechariah 7.10). The prophet Jonah powerfully reveals the compassion of the Father for the pagan non-believer in Nineveh and issues a harsh rebuke to God's people for their misunderstanding of the missionary nature of God. Jonah's decision to run from God's call to preach to the sinful Ninevites is held up as an example of what happens when privilege turns to prejudice and pride. Jonah could not fathom a God who did not share his prejudice, a God who was more generous and extravagant in love than he could grasp.

Even after his dark night of the soul deep within the belly of the fish and his subsequent obedience to God (and by all accounts a highly successful mission trip to Nineveh), Jonah remains out of touch with the heart of God. In the final chapter of the book, positioning himself outside the now repentant city of Nineveh, Jonah sulks, disappointed in the lack of hellfire and brimstone falling upon Nineveh, fearing the God of Israel might be a soft touch after all. Frustrated that the vine God had grown over him in the midday Middle Eastern sun has now withered, Jonah cannot see the irony of his own situation. Like the elder son who similarly positions himself outside the celebrations with the fatted calf, begrudging the mercy the father has shown to his younger brother, Jonah has failed to understand the nature of God. And so the book of Jonah ends with a profound question offered by God himself, 'And should I not be concerned about Nineveh, that great city?' (Jonah 4.11).

Jonah, the elder brother in the parable, and the Pharisees who question Jesus, have all failed to grasp that the love of God is more extravagant and generous than their religious framework has allowed. God's kindness has always been for those beyond the covenant also, for those who, like Nineveh, are lost and face judgement, because God's plans for salvation extend to the ends of the earth.

The love of God for the world reaches its fulfilment in the sending of his only Son. The events that we remember and celebrate during Holy Week point towards a God who is extravagant and persistent in his love for us. An innocent Saviour on a cross for sinners declares fully and triumphantly the extraordinary love of God for the world he made.

Extraordinary love for ordinary people

My husband has worked for many years as a GP in South London. In this vibrant part of the city he sees his missional calling to show compassion to those who are often at the very bottom of the pecking order (the lost, the least and the lawbreaker). He is keen for his patients to know that he is a Christian and so he has on his surgery wall a small picture that has 1 Peter 5.7 written on it, which says 'He Cares for You'. Unfortunately one day an elderly patient with failing eyesight came to see him and stared with horror at this picture. She had misread it and thought it said, 'He Comes for You!' which is probably the last thing you want to read at the GP's.

The message of the Bible is that God does indeed care. Evangelism finds its origin in God's extraordinary love and care for ordinary people; a love that is extravagant and unceasing in its persistence and devotion. It could be good to spend time this Lent asking, who are the lost people in our communities? Who are those we walk past each day without a second thought? Who are the down-trodden, the marginalized and the oppressed? The love of God is not only for them, but it is especially for them.

A group of people from my church regularly visit the local prison to take a Sunday service there. The stories of openness to faith and hunger for prayer and encounter with Jesus are astonishing to hear. One Sunday was particularly special. The singing in the prison chapel is always heartfelt but on this day something remarkable happened. The men's singing during the final verse of 'When I Survey' was especially loud and tuneful, with accompanying harmonies, and it seemed to the person leading the worship that it was as if an angelic host was singing along. After the service all those who had been involved in leading the worship shared their experience of what they had heard: each one of them had heard what sounded like a heavenly choir singing along with them. In this gathering of the lost, the least and the lawbreaker, the Spirit of God was clearly present and at work. God's heart is always for such as these and our role as witnesses is to follow where God the great missionary leads us, even to some of the forgotten and neglected corners of our society.

The record of the early Church indicates that Christ's love was both an intellectual conviction and a compelling incentive for evangelism among the early believers. Paul writes, 'For the love of Christ urges us on' (2 Corinthians 5.14). Evangelism begins with the intellectual conviction that God is love and that this love is extravagant and is extended to all who are the lost, the least and the lawbreaker. However, evangelism can never be purely about head knowledge; our witness is also rooted in our own experience of God's love and in the indwelling of the Spirit who pours God's love into our hearts (Romans 5.5).

One of the best examples of this irresistible compulsion by the love of God is when Peter and John are taken before the Sanhedrin in Acts 4 and they are forbidden from speaking any more about Jesus. Their response is to say, 'we cannot keep from speaking about what we have seen and heard' (Acts 4.20). Their experience of Christ's love was so real that they couldn't help but tell others about it. When have you ever had to tell a new Christian to evangelize? I remember a conversation with a friend of mine who had recently come to faith. He said, 'Oh, I'm not going to be one of *those* people who are really into evangelism, but the strange thing is, since I have become a Christian I can't stop talking to people about it.'

Somewhere there is a mismatch in our thinking between our perception of evangelism as something coercive, hard and socially awkward, and simply sharing the love of God with people. The starting point for evangelism, then, is not from a place of duty or obedience, since evangelism fashioned in the likeness of duty will easily run dry or lack sincerity, but God's love. Pope Francis expresses this beautifully in an exhortation entitled *Evangelii Gaudium*, which means 'The Joy of the Gospel':

The primary reason for evangelizing is the love of Jesus which we have received, the experience of salvation which urges us to ever greater love of him . . . If we do not feel an intense desire to share this love, we need to pray insistently that he will once more touch our hearts . . . What then happens is that "we speak of what we have seen and heard" (1 Jn 1:3). The best incentive for sharing the Gospel comes from contemplating it with love, lingering over its pages and reading it with the heart. If we approach it in this way, its beauty will amaze and constantly excite us . . . we have been entrusted with a treasure which makes us more human and helps us to lead a new life. There is nothing more precious which we can give to others.[2]

It would be great to make reflecting upon the love of Jesus for the world a focus of your study and prayer during the period of Lent. You can't spend time reading the Gospels and not be compelled by the love of Christ for the people around you. Perhaps a helpful discipline this Lent might be reading one of the Gospels and 'lingering over its pages and reading it with the heart'. Evangelism begins with glimpsing God's heart for the least, the lost and the lawbreaker.

God's heart for the lost

Hudson Taylor, the founder of the China Inland Mission in 1865, records in his journal an occasion when he was dressing the wound of a dying atheist man, known for his refusal to talk about the Christian faith. After several times of seeing to this man's gangrenous wounds, Hudson Taylor could hold in no longer his compulsion to speak to the man of the love of God and to offer to pray for him. Moved by the demonstration of passion, the man listened as Hudson Taylor, through his tears, shared the good news of Jesus. In time, this man too came to both know and experience the revolutionary love of God of which Hudson Taylor spoke. Reflecting later in his journal, Hudson wrote:

I have often thought since in connection with this case and the work of God generally of the words, 'He that goes forth weeping, bearing precious seed, shall doubtless come again rejoicing, bringing his sheaves with him.' Perhaps if we had more of that intense distress for souls that leads to tears, we should more frequently see the results we desire. Sometimes it may be that while we are complaining of the hardness of the hearts of those we are seeking to benefit, the hardness of our own hearts and our own feeble apprehension of the solemn reality of eternal things may be the true cause of our lack of success.[3]

In my own life I have experienced something of what Hudson Taylor talks about on a couple of occasions. One was rather embarrassingly my first Valentine's Day with my husband when we went to see *Titanic* at the newly opened local cinema. What I assumed would be a lovely romantic evening ended up being a profound experience of an encounter with the God who loves the lost, the least and the lawbreaker. Through the film God showed me his heart for the lost, both friends I knew and those I didn't. As bodies started to fall into the icy sea, God spoke to me about his heart for those who did not yet know him. I started to weep in the cinema, which wasn't that noticeable, as others were teary-eyed around me, but as the credits rolled I continued to weep. In the car journey home I could not control the tears and, arriving home, I lay on the bed and wept and prayed for a further two hours, leaving my poor husband wondering what had happened to his Valentine's Day. Sometimes it is only in the place of prayer where we see the people around us as the lost, the least and the lawbreaker. We may not view the colleague at the desk next to us or the school friend in these terms. However, reading the parables of Jesus reveals to us his extraordinary love for all who are far from him. Praying for God's heart for our friends and neighbours is a good place to start.

Love as motivation not manipulation

Evangelism, therefore, finds its origin in God's love for the lost, the least and the lawbreaker. However, we must be cautious in the way love is expressed in evangelism. As David Watson, the great

C of E evangelist in the 1970s, asked, 'Do you love people because you want to see them converted or do you want to see them converted because you love people?'[4] Love when employed incorrectly can be coercive and manipulative in evangelism. It is possible to engage in what we might call 'hit and run' or 'drive-by' evangelism. It's relatively easy to turn up on our local estate for a 'mission week', clearing up litter, handing out free food, getting into conversation about Jesus. It's relatively easy to post an evangelistic tract through every door of a block of flats. Such events might seem to get maximum coverage and impact. But what of love? How is love demonstrated in the one-off acts of the Church? Where are we months and years down the road for some of these forgotten communities? Even friendship can be used manipulatively if we think our friendship buys the right to speak about Jesus, or if we forge friendships in order to get people to come to church. Jesus' love wasn't just for those who would give up everything and follow, it was even for Judas who betrayed him at the very supper where Jesus had so clearly demonstrated his love for his disciples.

In 2015 my family and I took a three-month family trip to Uganda with CMS. My husband worked in the diocesan medical clinic and I did some lecturing in the theological college in Mukono. I loved teaching theology out in the open, aware of the background rustling, as monkeys swung through the branches of the mango trees overhead. As we suspected, we fell head over heels in love with Uganda, its climate, its vibrant colours and, most of all, its people. The Christmas we spent there with very few presents, no electricity due to a power cut but a wonderful celebration of food, dancing and prayer with our Ugandan host family was definitely voted 'best Christmas ever' by the kids. We left Uganda that spring with tears in our eyes knowing that we had received far more than we had given in this experience.

Three years later we could bear the absence no longer and so decided to return for a shorter trip in the summer holidays. When we arrived in Mukono, once again our host family greeted us with celebration, prayers and singing as they did every guest who arrived. They directed us through the place where we would be

I love people because[42] God asks us to love our neighbor as ourselves staying and we noticed the table was laid with beautiful linen and our favourite food of matoke (a savoury banana wrapped in leaves) and chicken was piping hot and waiting for us. The walls were surrounded with handmade posters with our names on them, celebrating our return. It was humbling to say the least and I thanked our host for going to so much trouble. The mama of the household turned to me and said, 'When you left three years ago, you said that you would return, but we did not believe you. Now that you have come back, we know that you love us.'

Sometimes the true test of our love for someone is when they tell us they are not interested in our faith, but we do not waiver in our love for them and the friendship remains. Evangelism that is primarily motivated by a crisis of decline will ultimately not reflect the one of whom the gospel so powerfully speaks. Love as a motivation in evangelism is rooted in God's love for the world, which is love for the long haul, love that is costly and committed and love that is ultimately sacrificial: 'For God so loved the world that he gave his only Son, so that everyone who believes in him may not perish but may have eternal life' (John 3.16). Our witness is always and only ever in response to the initiative of love that God shows the world in Christ. Where he has poured out his love, we follow in witness.

2 The need to trust God's work

There is another story Jesus told, which teaches us something important as we explore evangelism: the parable of the sower. Like many of Jesus' agricultural parables this demonstrates the somewhat unpredictable growth of the kingdom of God. Jesus' parables teach us about life in the kingdom and how its standards are often topsy-turvy to the principles and values of the culture around us. Like the mustard seed, which starts small and grows to a vast tree, the kingdom of God grows in unexpected and sometimes out-of-proportion ways. However, the parable of the sower indicates that not all the seeds sown have such a dramatic effect. Some seeds fall on the pathway, eaten by the birds before even having a chance to grow. Others fall on shallow soil and show initial promise but wither away under the midday sun. Still others seem to grow well but are eventually overrun by weeds; they don't die but they don't bear much quality grain. Finally there is the seed sown on the fertile ground which produces a harvest, some of which is way beyond mathematical multiplication.

In this parable, Jesus teaches us something significant about the unpredictable nature of evangelism. The seed is God's word which is sown liberally; the harvest is the fruitfulness of discipleship. The idea of sowing as a metaphor for evangelism is one that Paul also uses when talking about sharing the gospel with people:

You have heard of this hope before in the word of the truth, the gospel that has come to you. Just as it is bearing fruit and growing in the whole world, so it has been bearing fruit among yourselves from the day you heard it and truly comprehended the grace of God.
(Colossians 1.5–6)

The parable of the sower is a brilliant illustration of the reality of evangelism. It seems to parallel what we see in the ministry of Jesus. The seed is sown liberally, far and wide. In fact, you might be tempted to think that the sower is being a bit too extravagant. Why sow the seed on the pathway or the rocky ground? Surely that is just being careless? However, there is no hint of chastisement for the sower who sows the seed in this extravagant way. This is not considered a waste of seed but rather an inevitability of the seed being sown generously and without hesitation. This gentle and generous sowing is what we see in the ministry of Jesus. Jesus' ministry is initiatory rather than coercive, offered rather than demanded, extensive rather than limited. Just as the sower in the parable reaps a variety of responses, so too does Jesus. There are some who reject him outright, some who stay for a time but then walk away, and those who far outweigh expectations, leading others to know Jesus also. The parable of the sower is perhaps the most realistic teaching on evangelism we could be given; like Jesus, we too will receive a mixed response as we seek to share the good news of the kingdom.

Evangelism as partnership

In my second year at university we were given two huge boxes of Luke's Gospel to give out to students as part of the university mission week. One other girl and I set upon the task of knocking on 200 doors in college and offering people a copy of Luke's Gospel and an opportunity to talk about who Jesus was. Most people were reasonably polite, either taking one or saying no thank you; some even stopped and engaged us in conversation. Towards the end of the evening I knocked on the door of a final-year geography student I didn't know at all. He took the Gospel from me, instantly dropped it in the bin and shut the door in my face. Some months later, that same guy turned up at one of our enquirers' courses because his girlfriend had become a Christian. During subsequent weeks he too became a Christian and the last I heard of him was that he was thinking of becoming a vicar. I am glad that Jesus told his disciples a story about the unpredictable nature of evangelism, the importance of sowing widely but of not feeling downtrodden by the variety of responses.

Paul also uses the image of the sower to describe the work of evangelism:

> What then is Apollos? What is Paul? Servants through whom you came to believe, as the Lord assigned to each. I planted, Apollos watered, but God gave the growth. So neither the one who plants nor the one who waters is anything, but only God who gives the growth.
> (1 Corinthians 3.5–7)

Here Paul highlights the communal nature of evangelism; we do not do this alone. In many ways this is a refreshing rebuttal of our tendency to imagine evangelism as a lonely activity. I suspect that part of our current fear about it is influenced by the unhelpful image of the lonely evangelist speaking words of judgement through a megaphone on a street corner while shoppers walk on by. Even Paul, arguably one of the most confident evangelists there has ever been, recognized he couldn't do it on his own. He humbly points out to the Corinthians that even if he was the one to sow the initial seed, it was Apollos who watered the seed and, more importantly, it is God who gives the growth. It is in this way that we are reminded that evangelism is never individualistic but always done in partnership with others, and most importantly with God.

Joining in with God

One of the phrases most commonly associated with the term *missio Dei* is this: mission is finding out what God is doing and joining in. I have to confess that I have a somewhat love–hate relationship with this phrase. On the one hand it seems presumptuous to suggest that we get to join in with God's work in evangelism. When Jesus meets with the spiritual seeker Nicodemus in the darkness of night, their conversation makes clear the miraculous nature of evangelism. Becoming a disciple of Jesus is a matter of new birth. As Jesus says:

> No one can enter the kingdom of God without being born of water and Spirit. What is born of the flesh is flesh, and what is born of the Spirit is spirit. Do not be astonished that I said to you, 'You must be born from above.'
> (John 3.5–7)

In one sense, life in the kingdom is completely out of our hands. It is not ours to engineer or to grant to others. The gospel is a gift that we receive. It is God the great missionary who is ultimately at work and not us. However, Paul indicates that not only does he work in partnership with other ministers of the gospel but he also works in partnership with God. As Paul writes in 2 Corinthians 6.1: 'As we work together with him, we urge you also not to accept the grace of God in vain.' Paul understood himself as not only working for God in evangelism but with him also. This is what it means to say that mission is about joining in with what God is doing.

As witnesses, one of our first tasks in evangelism is to be on the lookout for the ways that God is already at work. In my experience with the hairdresser, I found myself in the situation where

I was playing catch-up to the work of God in someone's life. God had got there before me; my role as the witness was to add words and language towards what God was already doing. I wonder how this perspective might change our approach to conversations with people? How can we become better at looking for the ways that God is already at work? It may not always be as obvious as someone sharing an experience they had in church. Many will not even walk into a church building. However, we can discern God at work in someone's life even as we sense their openness to talk about deeper and more personal issues, their willingness to hunger and search for truth.

Never alone

Many of our fears about evangelism are because we think that we are alone in it. We are fearful of getting into conversations on our own with people in case they suddenly ask us questions about suffering or other things we don't have an answer to. We imagine that evangelism is something done on our own, outside the safety of the Church. It is as if we imagine we have been sent out on a solo mission like the soldier from *1917* with which we began this chapter. However, *missio Dei* reminds us that we are never on our own as witnesses to the risen Jesus. Whenever we point people towards Jesus in word and deed we are part of that which God is doing within the world. When the people of Israel welcomed the foreigners in their midst, they were being the display people they were meant to be; they were playing their part in salvation history, fulfilling God's intention that all nations should be blessed through them. Every time we point someone to Jesus in conversation, testimony, prayer or our lifestyle, we co-operate with the ministry that Paul points to, of bringing all things in heaven and on earth together under one head, even Christ (Ephesians 1.10). In this way, our attempts to engage in evangelism are always and only secondary to that which God is already doing.

The parable of the sower can reassure us that even some of our best attempts at sharing our faith are only worth something if the God of the harvest is at work by his Spirit, and that perhaps even some of our misguided best intentions can be turned into something fruitful by the one who alone can bring growth and breathe life where there is none.

Richard did not grow up in a Christian family and didn't consider himself particularly open to talking about faith. However, he used to meet up regularly with Owen, a friend from primary school, when they were both working in London. On one occasion they went for a drink in a pub and as they sat there with full pints of beer in front of them, Richard noticed Owen shifting awkwardly in his seat in front of him. As if out of nowhere Owen blurted out, 'Richard, erm, Jesus wants you to know that he loves you!' There was a stunned silence as they stared awkwardly at one another, not quite comprehending what had happened. Owen mumbled something about having to do something and he left the pub in haste, likely in embarrassment, leaving Richard sitting bemused at his table with two full pints of beer. As far as sensitive evangelism goes, this was pretty disastrous by all accounts. However, as Richard sat there in the pub he started to wonder what must be so important about Jesus and his love that his friend had gone to such lengths out of his comfort zone to communicate this message to him. This began Richard's own journey to faith and he started to explore Christianity. Over a period of time he came to know that Jesus really did love him and that risking social embarrassment was worth it to share this love with others. Even in our most awkward moments, God is still at work. He is the God of the harvest – not us. It is we who work in partnership with him and the success of evangelism does not ultimately rest upon our skill or our abilities but upon the work of the Spirit and the God of grace.

Prayer

It is because evangelism rests upon the work of the Spirit that prayer is so important. Prayer is the unglamorous and unseen work of witness, but it is the engine that provides the power. My friend James had been praying for his friend Rob every day for 15 years. After a while he started to run out of things to pray for and didn't know what to say, but each day he simply brought his friend Rob before the Lord in prayer and offered him to God. It was after

15 years of this daily prayer that Rob started asking big questions about the meaning of life and eventually decided to follow Jesus. There may be people you have been praying for for longer than 15 years, and yet the parable of the sower reminds us that we must keep on persevering and praying because God has not yet finished his work. There may be people in your community whom you have not yet started to pray for. Before rushing on to the next chapter, take time to pause and to reflect and ask God whom he would like you to pray for and commit to make them part of your regular prayers this Lent. It's so often been the case in my life that when I have been prayerful for someone or have prayed in advance of meeting someone, I am more likely to see the ways in which God has been at work in their lives. Jesus told his disciples, 'Ask, and it will be given to you; search, and you will find; knock, and the door will be opened for you' (Matthew 7.7). We are to be those who ask, search and knock so that others might also seek and discover the extraordinary love God has for them.

The parables Jesus taught have a lot to teach us about this unpredictable task of witnessing. There is much we can learn from his teaching that God is the initiator and that we are to trust the work of his Spirit in evangelism. However, as witnesses Jesus calls us to share the story of his work in our life through ordinary conversations, and it is to this that we will now turn.

For discussion

1 Have you ever felt you were just the person God wanted in a particular situation? Did later events confirm that in some way?
2 How do you think you might become more aware of God at work in relationships and conversations you are involved in?
3 Who might be regarded as 'the least', 'the lost' and 'the law-breaker' in your community, area, workplace (or even closer to home)?

3

Jesus was in the transformation business

How personal stories can authenticate the gospel for others

'Go home to your friends, and tell them how much the Lord
has done for you, and what mercy he has shown you.'
(Mark 5.19)

I am a sucker for a DIY programme on TV. You know the type.
Someone buys a house at auction; the first time they see it, usually
on a rainy day, there is an audible gasp as they view the wreck –
broken windows, nicotine-stained ceilings, carpets that look like a
health hazard. But in less than a year they have completely transformed it. Cue sunny weather and emotional music and smiles
all round. You can imagine my excitement when a few years
ago a friend of mine featured on an episode of *Homes Under the
Hammer*, only in her case when the TV crew came back a year later
they hadn't done quite as much as they were supposed to and the
house was only in a semi-transformed state. They got there in
the end, but transformation took a while.

Read through the Gospels and you will see Jesus is also in the
transformation business. Sometimes the transformation happens
instantly – as in the case of the paralysed man who after only a
word from Jesus picks up his mat and leaps away, knowing his sins
have also been forgiven. At other times the transformation is more
gradual. Take the example of impetuous Peter, who leaves behind
his fishing nets to follow Jesus but then repeatedly gets it wrong,
sometimes trying to stand in the way of what Jesus wants to do,

even denying him on the night of his arrest. However, Peter is one of the first witnesses to the resurrection and becomes the confident preacher at Pentecost. Consider John, the 'Son of Thunder', who wanted to call hellfire down on a town for not believing in Jesus. He became called 'the Apostle of Love' and was the one to whom Jesus entrusted his mother as he hung on the cross (John 19.26–27). Jesus is in the business of transformation but the transformation does not always happen overnight.

A story of transformation

One of the most remarkable stories of instant transformation is in Jesus' dealings with the demoniac in Mark 5. Jesus travels by boat to an area called the land of the Gerasenes. It is one of the first encounters that we see Jesus having in Gentile territory. In this remote place, Jesus encounters a man who is possessed by multiple demons. The initial description that Mark gives us of this man is distressing: wild and unkempt, ostracized from the local community, even his own family, wailing out loud and a danger to himself. We can only presume that this troubled man had no prior knowledge of Jesus, yet he is drawn to him and falls down on his knees before him. It becomes clear that the man is entirely riddled with demons and that only the all-powerful word of Jesus can break his chains. Jesus instantly sets the man free, although it does not turn out so well for the herd of pigs nearby. Mark is keen to report that by the time the crowd had heard of this story they were faced with an entirely different picture of the man, who now sat clothed, calm and able to communicate articulately. The transformation undergone by this man was complete: from chaos to peace, from danger to security.

This miracle is one of many instances in the Gospels when encounter with Jesus brings complete and utter transformation and freedom. You might think that this story of transformation would be met with great relief by the town who no longer have to listen to the terrifying screams of the man wandering around the tombs. However, their fear now turns away from this man and focuses on Jesus instead. They are unsure what to make of his power and were possibly also concerned about the impact on the local farming community. The town turns out and begs Jesus to leave. This is so different from the many occasions where people beg Jesus to stay. Here his presence is not welcome. It is therefore not surprising that the freed man now wants to follow the one who has set him free. Why stay in the town that has exiled him? The man tries to climb in the boat with Jesus when he goes to leave, but Jesus says these words to him: 'Go home to your friends, and tell them how much the Lord has done for you, and what mercy he has shown you' (Mark 5.19).

It is surprising that Jesus doesn't take the man with him, isn't it? Only a few chapters ago he had been recruiting followers for his newly formed band of disciples. Surely this man would be the perfect new apprentice with a miraculous story to share? Jesus knows the home crowd are hostile. Why not save the man the hardship and take him on board? However, Jesus resists the man's desire to follow him and instead sends him back as a witness to his own community, the very community that had been so fearful of him. What is also striking is that this man has very little experience of Jesus other than this one exchange. He hasn't listened to the hours of teaching that the other disciples had. However, Jesus sends him back, simply to tell 'how much the Lord has done' for him. This man was called to witness to the story of God's work in his life, to speak of his utter transformation and his present experience of freedom and peace. And we soon read that 'everyone was amazed' in the surrounding towns (Mark 5.20). Where Jesus had caused initial confusion and fear, this man's story of his encounter with Jesus in turn began to transform the lives around him.

I love this story from Mark's Gospel because it is a powerful illustration of the influence of personal story. Jesus leaves the man in his home town, untrained but full of his own personal encounter. And the results speak for themselves. This way of witnessing is one of the first and easiest ways we can start to share our faith with people, and can be one of the simplest ways to get started on imaginative evangelism.

The power of personal story

Our culture today is fascinated by the story of individuals. Each Saturday *The Guardian* features an article called 'Experience', which focuses on the story of an ordinary individual who has a tale to tell about their life. These stories range from the near miraculous – the man who survived 76 days adrift a raft on the Atlantic Ocean – to the inspiring stories of the amputee who trained to be a professional tap dancer on stage. Some stories make you weep with the ordeals that people face in life, such as the man who spent 28 years imprisoned on death row in America for a crime he didn't commit. Others are more humorous or bizarre: the professional eater who holds the record for eating 501 chicken wings in 30 minutes, or the man who narrated his experience of his 76-mile crossing of the Alps on a space hopper. The point is, anyone is free to write in and share their story and we, the reader, are irresistibly drawn by them. We have become great narrators of our own personal experiences as this *Guardian* column shows. The rise of blogs, podcasts and vlogs also shows how fascinated we are by personal stories. We are intrigued by successful TV programmes such as *Long Lost Family*, where we are drawn into the discovery of someone's family and their personal journey. In journalism the way to engage people with a complex issue in the media is often to focus in on one individual. No one can forget the huge wave of public response at the tragic photo of the little Syrian refugee, Alan Kurdi, whose body was found on the shore of a beach in Turkey in 2015. It is sometimes the focus on the human story that provides a gateway to understanding the larger and more complex narrative.

In the book of Acts the first disciples witnessed to the facts of the resurrection but they were not afraid to put their personal story to the complex narrative of the gospel. They preached powerfully and persuasively about the Scriptures but they also shared their experience of personal encounter with the risen Jesus. When standing before the Sanhedrin, accused of disturbing the peace with their proclamation of the risen Jesus and the miraculous healings, Peter and John are not afraid to make it personal: 'we cannot keep from speaking about what we have seen and heard' (Acts 4.20). At this point Peter and John do not seek to offer a rational defence of the resurrection but instead are compelled to offer their own experience, what they have seen with their eyes and heard with their ears. In a similar way, the Apostle Paul repeatedly refers to his own story of encounter on the road to Damascus. He writes about it in his letters and presents it as his defence in some of the most serious situations, not least when he is on trial in Jerusalem. What Jesus knew when he sent the newly liberated man of the Gerasenes back to his home town was that story is powerful.

Sharing your story

Everyday witness involves sharing our own personal story with people. Even in our postmodern culture where there is suspicion of metanarratives that seek to provide overarching answers to all people and places, little stories have a powerful voice; they can connect and provide a way into the bigger story. Our personal experience often authenticates and earths the gospel message for people. Our story can be a particularly effective way of connecting with people in a culture that values experience more highly than truth. In my own experience of evangelism I have noticed this subtle shift over more recent years. Friends seem less interested in classic apologetic questions such as 'Can I trust the Bible?' or 'Do all religions lead to God?' Instead, their position is more often one of unfamiliarity with the Christian faith rather than objections against it, but they are, however, interested in the personal story. What difference does being a Christian make to the way I bring up my children or spend my money? How did being a Christian affect the way I viewed the Brexit debate or might vote at the next election? These are all topics of conversations I have found myself having over the last couple of years, in which being able to put my name to 'his' story has been significant. When we share our story we do not position ourselves as authorities on the faith, but as learners, experiencers, and as those who are on a journey. John Drane expresses it like this:

When we preach sermons, or hand on ready-made summaries of Christian belief and theology, we inevitably present ourselves as experts. Doing it that way, it is all but impossible to avoid giving the impression that we are people who have it all together, people with no questions. But when we tell stories, we reveal ourselves as weak and vulnerable – spiritual pilgrims with whom others can identify.

As followers of Jesus we all have our own unique story to tell. We all have an 'I have seen' story we can share.

Lara grew up in a nominally Roman Catholic home. While she didn't attend church as a child she remembers her mum praying with her the following prayer at night: 'If I should die before I wake, O grant the Lord my soul to take.' At the time, this frightened Lara and initially ideas of God were intermingled with belief in the tooth fairy, Santa and the Easter bunny. When she grew older and began to question those things, her Mum assured her that out of all of them God was real, but it had little impact on the way Lara viewed her everyday life and if anything it was tinged with the initial fear she had felt as a young child. But her childhood was happy and she had a good relationship with her parents growing up.

When Lara was 13 her mum started attending their local church (which the family jokingly called the 'happy clappy church'). Lara noticed a change in her mum as she was full of joy for her newly rediscovered faith and spoke of God in much more personal ways. Lara tried the church a few times but it didn't really connect with her and she left all thoughts of church behind as she moved to university on the South Coast at 18.

At university Lara hit the party scene hard. She began dating someone who was really into clubbing, drinking and drugs, and she found herself at the heart of the party scene. She lost interest in her academic course and her life became focused on partying and drugs, which started to have a detrimental effect upon her mental health and well-being. At that time her dad was diagnosed with oesophageal cancer. This had an enormous impact on Lara but the pressure of being upbeat every time she came home to see her dad, whose condition was rapidly deteriorating, meant that she didn't let on to her family the struggles she was going through.

She faced other tragedies and bereavements that year, and when her relationship with her boyfriend also came to an end Lara felt herself plummeting into depression and anxiety, and she started to withdraw from her network of friends. Remarkably her dad went into remission the following year, but Lara didn't want to bring her family down with her own troubles and so kept them hidden away from them and began to develop an eating disorder.

Lara's mum's faith continued to be an anchor for the whole family although at the time she was the only believer. She would send Lara Bible verses and worship songs which Lara would ignore.

Lara sensed she was at a crisis point in her life and so started to seek help from a counselling service provided by the university. One of the struggles Lara faced was insomnia and she often found herself walking along the seafront alone at night. Late one evening Lara felt at her absolute lowest and walked down to the beach feeling inside that life had to be more than just waiting for the next bad thing to happen. The beach was entirely deserted and she was in complete darkness apart from the moonlight shimmering on the water. She cried out to God, saying, 'God, if you are there I need you to show up. I need you to give me something to live for.' She heard a voice in her head telling her to turn around. She looked behind her and saw a man that she presumed to be homeless slowly trudging his way through the sand pushing a shopping trolley. Again Lara heard this voice in her head saying, 'That's what you are living for' and Lara had this sudden realization that she had made her life all about herself, what she looked like and what party she would go to. Instinctively, she ran back to the house and made a cup of tea for this man struggling his way through the sand. It was a small gesture, but she sensed this was somehow symbolic of the change in direction her life was now taking. Lara didn't tell anyone about her mysterious encounter on the beach and she started to wonder if that had been God speaking to her. She dug out the Bible verses that her mum had sent her and started listening to the worship songs online.

A week later she received a social media message from someone she had met six years previously who simply said, 'Lara, I know this is going to sound really weird but do you want to come to church with me on Sunday?' Lara agreed to attend with her the following Sunday. Lara's first experience of church was pretty overwhelming. It was a megachurch with lots of noise and loud worship, quite unlike anything she had experienced before. However, she met her friend (who was grinning from ear to ear!) and sat with her through the whole service. The person preaching spoke of the love of God and asked if anyone wanted to receive Christ into their lives to come up to the front. Lara felt herself getting up from her seat and walking forward to the front before she could realize what was happening to her. As someone started to pray with her she began to cry uncontrollably as a sense of love washed over her and she felt unconditionally loved in a way she had never experienced before in her life. It was a sense of love that held her and made her feel life would be different, that life would be okay with Jesus. Lara went back to the church again later in the week and was prayed for again, and again she encountered the tangible love of Christ and experienced the Spirit setting her free from many of the battles and struggles she was facing. Those praying for her were slightly taken aback by her rather loud announcement that this was more incredible than any high she had experienced taking drugs.

From this moment onwards things started to really change in Lara's life. She got back on board with her academic work, started attending a local church and soaked up all the teaching and discipleship she could get. She grew in confidence in her identity and sense of renewed purpose in life. The previous impression Lara had of God as somehow frightening or distant was replaced by an awareness of unconditional love and peace. Her priorities started to change and she no longer needed to be the party girl to fulfil her hunger for acceptance. She grew more and more secure in her belief that what she experienced that night in church was not a random experience but the beginning of her journey as a loved and cherished child of God. Over time she started to hear God speaking to her about her future, that she was being called to live her life in the service of others as she had felt that night on the beach. Lara is now training for ordination in the Church of England, with a passion for leading other young adults like herself to know the transformative power of the unconditional love of God.

We all have a story to share

We all have our own story of the way that God has worked in our life. Like our thumbprint, which is unique to us, so is the story of our faith journey. Yours might not be as dramatic as Lara's but it is nevertheless a story of God's grace and presence. My own testimony is more gradual but it is still one that I frequently share in conversation with people. So how do we share our story with others? How do we follow in the footsteps of the man in Mark 5 and 'stay and tell of what the Lord has done'. Here are some ideas that might help you consider how you can be a witness through sharing your own story.

Be prepared

It's always good to think through in advance what you might say to someone if they ask you why or how you became a Christian. Your story might fit neatly into the categories of before and after; there may be a clear moment in which you became a Christian, and it can be good to think about how you might tell that to someone. However, it might not fit so easily into those categories. You might have always been a Christian or your faith journey might have been more gradual over a long period of time. If that is your experience, then try to think how you would express to someone the difference that Jesus makes in your life. What is it about Jesus that particularly draws you to him? When have you experienced God at work in a difficult or tough period of your life?

Having an idea of what we might say to someone can really help with our confidence when the occasion arises. Being prepared and knowing what we might say frees us to be more present in the moment, being attentive to the person sitting before us rather than inwardly panicking about what our next sentence might be. I am not suggesting that you learn your story by rote and deliver it parrot fashion at every given opportunity, but being prepared is one of the best tools we have at our disposal in evangelism.

Be accessible

The longer you have been a Christian the harder it is to recognize the presence of Christian jargon. If you can remember back to becoming a Christian or first attending church, what are some of the words that you didn't understand? It can be difficult sometimes to comprehend how alien and odd things sound to people unfamiliar with the Christian faith and its concepts. At my youngest son's baptism a family with whom we are really good friends came to the church service. They are atheists and not at all used to going to church. However, when they walked into church during the first song I noticed their 7-year-old daughter was smiling from ear to ear. She told me later that they were singing her song. We had been singing a song with the word 'Hosanna' repeatedly during the chorus but since her name was Rosanna she assumed the church was singing to welcome her in. If only everyone received such a joyful and personal welcome! However, the reality is that much of the language we use is strange and unfamiliar to people. I have often thought that the imagery of 'being washed in the blood of the lamb' must sound horrendous to the agnostic vegetarian who happens to turn up in church one day. That is not to say that we should shy away from talking about Christian concepts or patronize people with simplistic explanations; sometimes the ideas are so novel to people that they actually become curious. Instead what we need to do is be more aware of the language we take for granted as Christians and think about more accessible ways of explaining things.

When you have the opportunity to share your story with someone, try and avoid using 'in' language as much as possible. For example, the word 'sin' is often understood in a different way from the one we intend. Imaginative evangelism requires us to find alternative ways of expressing it: rebellion, brokenness, idolatry, missing the mark, messing up, falling short are all possibilities and probably easier for people to comprehend than 'sin', which feels outdated. Another example would be the word 'salvation', which we know is central to our faith. But, again, it is a word that has confusing or little meaning for people today. Instead I prefer to talk about rescue, being reconciled to God, being restored, forgiven or set free. These are all concepts that carry more resonance with people.

Be authentic

The story of how God has worked in your life is unique and you need to own it, warts and all. Sometimes we can feel intimidated if our story isn't the dramatic transformation testimony that we are used to hearing on the stage of the Christian conference. The reality is that most of us are pretty ordinary people and so our testimony is just what is needed. Within every ordinary story there will be the trace of the extraordinary. Learning to be ourselves in witness can be a huge step forward. We do not need to pretend to be someone else. We are not claiming to have all the answers but we are instead simply offering that we have found Jesus to be true, real, forgiving and transformative in our lives. This seems to be the approach that the Apostle John takes:

> We declare to you what was from the beginning, what we have heard, what we have seen with our eyes, what we have looked at and touched with our hands, concerning the word of life – this life was revealed, and we have seen it and testify to it, and declare to you the eternal life that was with the Father and was revealed to us – we declare to you what we have seen and heard.
> (1 John 1.1–3)

When we share our story with someone, we aren't claiming definitive proof, but we are saying that we have found something extraordinary and compelling that we want to share with others.

Be honest

Sometimes we can be tempted to pretend that following Jesus will make everything perfect in someone's life. Be honest about the struggles as well as the high points. When we share our story truthfully in this way we make ourselves vulnerable and therefore more approachable. While Jesus is in the transformation business and we have experienced that in our lives, there is no guarantee that following Jesus means we will have a life free from suffering. In fact some of the most powerful testimonies I have heard have been shared by those who have gone through the depths of sorrow and pain and yet have found Jesus to be present with them through it all. All we have to do is speak honestly of what we have 'seen and heard'.

Similarly, we don't have to pretend to be perfect – that can sometimes be more off-putting. When I lived as a student in a shared house with a number of people who weren't Christians they often used to call me out whenever I did anything wrong. I think that they presumed that because I was a Christian I would be perfect. Initially I found this frustrating because I was trying so hard to be a 'good witness' and yet was worried I was doing a terrible job. However, I realized in time that my role was not to be perfect but to point to Jesus, and I began to talk more openly about how as a Christian I knew that I made mistakes but that because of Jesus' death I had a fresh start and forgiveness. Those honest conversations ended up being more powerful than me pretending to be something I wasn't.

Be bold

Sharing our story with someone is a real privilege but it is simultaneously a huge responsibility. We want to say as much as we can without overloading people. This is where boldness comes in. It's easy to talk about spiritual experiences but when the disciples shared their testimony it was centred entirely on Jesus: his death on the cross and his resurrection from the dead. In sharing my testimony I always try to say something of what the death of Jesus means for me and of my hope that Jesus is alive today. Rowan Williams describes Easter as 'the one focal interpretive story of Jesus'.[1] We understand who Jesus is because he is the one who is risen from the dead. However, we also understand ourselves in the light of his resurrection. We live because he also lives. Our story, therefore, should always point to Jesus as its focal point, as the one who makes sense of who we are and how we live. When Jesus encountered the Samaritan woman at the well and she then went back to Samaria, all she had to speak of was her encounter with Jesus. Nevertheless we hear that 'many Samaritans from that city believed in him because of the woman's testimony' (John 4.39). The Samaritan woman was unashamed to speak of Jesus and what he had done for her – and because of it, many others came to believe. We never know how God will use our story in someone else's life, so be bold and ready to put Jesus at the centre. When I share my story with people the one thing I want them to remember is that I am really passionate about Jesus.

Be relevant

There is a tendency when we think about sharing our story with people to talk about what happened in the past but it's important to talk about our present reality of Jesus too and the difference he makes to the situations we encounter in our ordinary lives. A few years ago, we became caught up as a family in a really difficult situation which caused a lot of stress, hurt and pain. You might think that this kind of situation wouldn't be an easy one in which to witness, but we had some profound conversations with friends who could see what we were going through and asked us how we were coping. We were able to be honest and talk about our struggles but also talk about how our faith in Jesus was acting as an anchor to us, which led to some of the most open and honest conversations we have ever had with people. Sharing our testimony doesn't mean we have to pretend that life is a bed of roses when you follow Jesus, but even through the difficult times God is still at work, weaving his way through the story of our lives so that we can continue to speak of his extraordinary love for us.

When sharing our story with someone it can be important not just to talk about the events that happened but to focus on the difference that they make. You aren't simply narrating a sequence of events. What is it about being a Christian that particularly makes a difference for you? Perhaps it is the sense of peace that you know deep in your heart. Maybe it's the knowledge that you are not alone, or perhaps it's the relief that comes from knowing you are forgiven and loved. These themes of peace, security, acceptance and love can speak powerfully into people's lives and can in turn help them in their own search for meaning and truth.

Look for the connections

Evangelism isn't just about sharing our story. It's also about the story of the person sitting before us. And it's also about God's story and how he longs for people to enter into his story and make it theirs too. As we will see in the following chapter, Jesus does this masterfully. As with all witnessing, sharing our story should never be one-way traffic. As we speak we need to be prepared to listen to the other person's story also and to find points of connection with our own, and ultimately with God's story. When you have shared your story with someone it might be good to have some questions up your sleeve that you might ask afterwards. You could ask, 'How does what I have just shared compare with your idea of what a Christian is?' Or you might like to ask a question to invite something of their story. Asking questions is the best way to make the connection with someone's story. On the whole, people tend to like talking about themselves and so being curious about other people can open up significant conversations. As someone shares their story with you, acknowledge and value it. Developing the art of prayerful attention is effective in enabling you to listen to what God might be saying to the person as they talk. It's important to listen not just with our ears but with our eyes also, to give some-one our full attention. It is a privilege to be trusted with someone's story, particularly when they are being open about their struggles. Be sure to value and honour it and seek to find ways to connect their story with yours and ultimately with God's story.

Be respectful

It's important to be mindful of the person you are speaking to. You aren't delivering some pre-packaged spiel but engaging in conversation, so don't let it be too one-sided. It's not natural in conversations to speak at someone for ten minutes. In fact, we tend to avoid people who do that. You might like to begin by asking the question, 'Can I tell you something about my story of becoming a Christian?' or 'Can I tell you something about my spiritual journey?' Try to listen as well as speaking when you share your story, allowing the person space to comment or interject.

When someone shares their story with you they are entrusting you with something precious. We must be good stewards of the experiences of others and be careful not to manipulate them for our own advantage. This is where asking questions to determine whether someone wants you to share more with them can be helpful. If someone has shared an experience of loss, sorrow or pain, or a time of anxiety in their life, you don't need to pretend to be able to match their experience, but if there is something that you can relate to, you could ask a follow-up question such as, 'Can I tell you about a time when I felt really anxious about X but found a sense of peace?' However, we don't need to force it. Sometimes people are open to talking more but we need to become emotionally intelligent and read the signs when people have perhaps shared enough or where people want us to stop talking and simply listen. I am often reminded of the rich young ruler who walked away sad from Jesus because the cost was too high. I frequently wonder how Jesus must have felt in that moment. But Jesus didn't run after him and try and persuade him further; he didn't beg him to believe or shout and tell him he was making a mistake. All we are told is that he looked at him and loved him.

As we share our stories with people there will be those who are on the edge of their seat, wanting to know more. There will be others who are intrigued and might come back to us another day with a follow-up question. But there will be others who, like the rich young man, walk away. In each of these we have to trust that the God who has invited us into his story is inviting them also.

A story shared is a story lived

The story of God's work in our life can never purely be an exercise in retrospection. The story we share is the reality in which we now live, and our actions as well as our words are crucial in sharing our story with people. In writing to the church at Thessalonica, Paul reminds them how he behaved when he was with them:

64

As you know and as God is our witness, we never came with words of flattery or with a pretext for greed; nor did we seek praise from mortals, whether from you or from others, though we might have made demands as apostles of Christ. But we were gentle among you, like a nurse tenderly caring for her own children. So deeply do we care for you that we are determined to share with you not only the gospel of God but also our own selves, because you have become very dear to us. (1 Thessalonians 2.5–8)

Paul knew that the gospel story could never be communicated purely with words but it had to be lived as well. Our story becomes more authentic to people when they see that it really does have an impact on the way we live our lives. It is often through our daily lives that we demonstrate the topsy-turvy way of the kingdom of God. In a culture where people are more interested in whether things work than whether things are true, our lived experience becomes a potent advocate in our everyday witness.

Sophie grew up in a family who never attended church. She went to the local church school but it was never part of her home life and growing up she did not give much thought to the idea of religion or faith. As a teenager she called herself agnostic but she did start to explore questions of spirituality and wondered whether there was life after death. However, she didn't consider Christianity to have the answers to that; it seemed too mainstream. At the age of 19 she found herself living in a shared house with other young people. While she joined in with socializing and drinking she started to be increasingly aware of a void in her life. She carried on joining in with the crowd but there was a young woman called Emily in her house who seemed to have found a very different way of living. Sophie recalls that Emily seemed to have very different priorities; she went off to church on a Sunday and she would run a small group in their living room each week, which made Sophie curious. However, it wasn't just activities that made Emily seem different. Sophie found her to be consistently kind and caring, and never judgemental about some of Sophie's life choices that were clearly at odds with Emily's. In time Sophie began to ask questions about the Christian faith and they started talking together. At points Sophie became angry and would vehemently disagree with Emily. But on each occasion she was met with love and acceptance. Emily never claimed to know all the answers and there were some times she didn't know what to say to Sophie's next challenging question, but this made her seem more authentic in Sophie's book as she saw that her faith really was a part of her everyday life. In time Sophie was intrigued enough to attend an enquirers course where she became a Christian. However, it was the patient and loving witness of a Christian friend who didn't just talk the talk but walked it that had the greatest impact on Sophie's own story.

In one of his letters, Peter writes:

> but in your hearts sanctify Christ as Lord. Always be ready to make your defence to anyone who demands from you an account of the hope that is in you; yet do it with gentleness and reverence.
>
> (1 Peter 3.15–16)

This verse is often used to describe how we are to be engaged in apologetics, the task of presenting a defence of the Christian faith, but what is often overlooked in the verse is the reason that lies behind the question. Peter assumes that the way followers of Jesus are loving provokes questions in those around them, and that those questions are particularly about the hope that we have. There is an assumption that the way we live our lives will prompt people to ask questions. With Emily and Sophie that was definitely the case. Living his story is both public and authentic. It is not to be hidden away but lived authentically alongside people.

Living in the open

One of the legacies of the modern era was the presumption that religious faith was a matter of personal preference and therefore should not be present in the public sphere. As witnesses of Jesus, our faith is both private and public, both personal and corporate.

Jesus' followers were never to hide away but to live their lives publicly for all to see. However, this also presents a challenge to the way we live our lives as the Church today. It is all well and good to talk to people about the extraordinary love of God, but if people are struggling and in need then such words are hollow without action to accompany them. An emotional message about God's love cannot fill an empty stomach. As Jesus announced in the synagogue, his good news was for the blind, the poor and the oppressed. We cannot speak of the extraordinary love of God if we are not prepared to act in radical and sacrificial ways ourselves.

Brian Stone is a theologian who writes on the nature of evangelism in a pluralistic world. One of his main convictions is that evangelism points to a whole new way of life that is already being lived out by the Christian community. As those who seek to witness to Jesus Christ we also need to recognize that the way we live is an embodiment of the good news. The medium is also the message:

> The good news heralded by the church is that in Christ salvation is now possible in the form of a new way of life. This salvation is not an experience to be passively received or a set of propositions to be assented to. It really is a way to be embarked upon, a way we forgive each other's sins, a way we love and include those who are different from us, a way we welcome the poor, a way we love our enemies, a way we bind up those who are broken hearted or have suffered loss, a way we cancel debts, and a way the world's hierarchies are turned upside down in Christlike patterns of fellowship.[2]

As witnesses of Jesus we have a wonderful story of good news to tell but we also have a story to live. Living Jesus' story is costly and can be uncomfortable but there is no other way to live once you have encountered the risen Lord. Since the first Good Friday and Easter Sunday 2,000 years ago, disciples of Jesus have been discovering there is life in the story of Jesus. This life is opened up to us in the gospel of Jesus and we are privileged as those who get to share this story, through our story, with others. Evangelism is never just the story we tell. It is also the story we live.

'I have seen'

I love that in one of the first encounters we see Jesus having in the Gospels all he leaves behind is an individual with a story. The man from the Gerasenes went back to his home town with the story of Jesus' transformation on his lips. He had no knowledge of the Scriptures yet to explain to people, but he could speak powerfully of Jesus who had turned his life upside down and set him free. The changed appearance of the man was proof to those who listened that this Jesus he spoke of really was unlike anyone they had ever met before. On its own this story might not seem much. What can one person achieve, after all? On its own it might seem insignificant, but it is a story that became multiplied as others around this man started to enquire about who this Jesus is and whether he can do for them what he has done for the man with the story. In this way, those simple words 'I have seen' can become the beginning point of another person's story, and another and another.

For discussion

1 Think of a story of encountering God that you have shared with others or others have shared with you. What did you learn from the experience?
2 In what practical ways might you express God's love to a neighbour this week?
3 At this point in your Lenten journey, be still for a while and imagine Jesus gazing into your eyes in love. How do you find yourself responding?

4
Communicating like Jesus did

Learning how to have life-transforming conversations

A Samaritan woman came to draw water, and Jesus said to her, 'Give me a drink.'
(John 4.7)

People sometimes try to guess what kind of personality type Jesus was. Was he a 'yellow', inspiring people towards a new vision, a 'green', compassionate and empathetic for those in need?[1] Where would he fall on an Enneagram test: 9, a peacemaker, or 2, a helper? What Myers Brigg type would Jesus be? Those who are extroverts find themselves drawn to Jesus' relentless engagement with people; he frequently attends parties, sometimes even invites himself to them, and he allows himself to be distracted by stopping and talking with people on the way. Those of a more introvert persuasion cite the occasion Jesus leaves behind the crowd to find time to be alone with his Father and pray, the time he falls asleep on the boat, surely tired by so much human interaction; they cite his thoughtful teaching, his use even of silence at appropriate moments. It would seem Jesus is rather hard to put into a box.

However, one thing is clear as we read the Gospels and that is that Jesus knew how to engage with people. He was deeply personal in his approach and he cared about people. But he didn't treat everyone the same way. Some of us might have been brought up with quite fixed ideas about what we need to say to people when we talk about the gospel. Those of us from evangelical backgrounds might have learned simple gospel outlines to share with people. However, the problem with such approaches is that they can be rather generic, learned and recited without taking into consideration the individuals we might actually be talking to. Sometimes our simple explanations and answers don't seem to relate fully to the complex reality of the person sitting before us. What we need is better and more imaginative ways to connect the gospel we know and believe with the person we are talking to. This is the pressing task of Christian witness.

Everyday witness

Witness as a way of life is something we are all called to do in every aspect of our life. Witnessing flows naturally and purposefully out of the lives of those who live the gospel story in the world today. When we discover a new TV show we like we don't tend to think of a strategy of how to tell our friends about it. It bubbles up naturally in ordinary conversation. When we discover a new recipe that works and tastes good we don't need a strategy for how to introduce people to it, we simply invite our friends over and let them try it. Conversations about the things we love most and are most interested in arise naturally and easily through the connectedness of our lives with people that we know. The good news of Jesus is no different – it has always been passed on through ordinary individuals. Witnessing can take the form of discussions in the workplace, a family meal around the table, an unexpected conversation with a stranger in our GP's waiting room, a chat with a fellow parent at the school gates that starts a friendship.

This person-to-person approach is the one that Jesus advocates to his disciples. In Luke 10, when Jesus sends out the 72, he doesn't ask them to set up large public gatherings in the town square but rather to adopt a house-to-house approach: 'Remain in the same house, eating and drinking whatever they provide' (Luke 10.7). While Jesus sends out his disciples to preach, cast out demons and heal the sick, it is evident that personal relationships formed the bedrock of their ministry. Friendship is core to how we witness through our everyday lives and how we pass on the good news of God's love. Beautiful evangelism is so often born out of relationships and love. Stefan Paas is a Dutch theologian and one of the most stimulating thinkers exploring how the Church continues its witness in today's secular age. He suggests that the emphasis on relationships we observe in the ministry of Jesus and his disciples is of paramount importance in the way we engage in witness today:

> Essentially, it is nothing more than the fostering of natural human relationships, while being unembarrassed about the Christian faith. Or, in other words, it amounts to opening up our private lives for others, and talking about the deepest thoughts and feelings when the opportunity presents itself. Of course, this may very well be connected with more formal approaches of evangelism, such as the Alpha course or catechesis around baptisms and church weddings. The bottom line, however, is a rich vision of human togetherness in which we are not shy about what ultimately concerns us. This is the core practice of evangelism and nothing much will happen without it.[2]

Relationships are the bedrock of our everyday witness. We cannot witness to the good news of God's love if we are not spending time in the company of other people, particularly those outside the Church. The 'Talking Jesus' research discovered that the second most common way someone became a Christian was through having conversations with people who were Christians. This was second only to being brought up in a Christian family and came before attending church or reading the Bible.[3] Conversations are therefore a crucial part of what it means to be a witness.

We have tended to think of evangelism in terms of telling people about Jesus. What if we were not just to communicate what Jesus did but to communicate like Jesus did? There is so much we can learn from how Jesus interacted with people. The Gospels record over 150 one-to-one conversations that Jesus has with people. While Jesus' aim was always that of initiating people into the kingdom of God, he did this in so many different ways, in so many different places and with so many different people. When it comes to conversations, Jesus has much to teach us.

So, what can we draw from the way Jesus interacted with people? What does Jesus have to teach us about beautiful evangelism?

Jesus related to all different kinds of people

Spend time in the Gospels and you will soon discover that Jesus meets and mixes with all different kinds of people: fishermen, tax collectors, religious officials, mothers-in-law, young people, wealthy and rich, sick and well, those of highest rank and those of lowest regard, those who were for him and those who hated him. Jesus was in some sense indiscriminate in the way he spent his time. Jesus was often at the heart of social gatherings and parties.

However, there were those who criticized Jesus for this. Jesus alludes to the fact that he has been accused of being a 'glutton and a drunkard' for attending some of the parties he has been at (Matthew 11.19). In Luke 7 Jesus attends a banquet at the house of Simon the Pharisee where he welcomes the interruption by the 'sinful woman' who anoints his feet. In Luke 10, Jesus spends time at the home of two sisters, Mary and Martha, two friends that we presume he knew well from the boldness of Martha's interaction with him. Jesus also invited himself to Zacchaeus' house for a meal, once again facing the judgement of the crowd who disapproved of him being hosted by a 'sinner' (Luke 19.7). Early on in John's Gospel we meet Jesus at a wedding where he suddenly becomes the centre of attention as he turns water into wine. Jesus was a great guest to have at a party! As well as attending lots of parties, Jesus also told stories about them. Many parables have the image of a party to describe the joyful reality of life in his new kingdom (Luke 15.24).

For Christians this can challenge where and with whom we spend the majority of our lives. As someone who works for a living in the Church, I find Jesus' approach particularly unsettling. I once spoke about 'Jesus the evangelist' as a guest preacher at a church and afterwards a woman in her eighties came up to me and said, 'When you were talking I realized that I spend all my time at church events and with other Christians. I've decided this week to start attending the local lunch club and make some friends. I'm going to get a life!' For some of us the starting point in our journey towards living his story this Lent is simply making connections and friendships with those outside our church communities; taking longer at the school gates to stop and chat, inviting someone at work to have lunch or coffee together, checking in on elderly neighbours, joining a local sports club.

However, even when we have friends outside the Church, as Christians we can tend to operate in compartments in our life; over here are our church friends, and we do certain types of things with them, and over here are my non-church friends, and never the twain shall meet. But for Jesus, it was never that clear-cut. He allowed the sinful woman to interrupt the nice religious banquet. He invited himself to the house of the tax collector. He positioned himself deliberately and intentionally in mixed communities.

I have three sons who all love football. Naturally they have friends who also love football and we have found this to be a brilliant common gathering point within our community. We have now established a tradition of hosting a party to watch England's first match of any international tournament. We have purchased a projector and invite people to bring internationally themed food depending on who is playing that day. Our kids invite their friends, and even the parents of their friends, and we invite a mix of people we know from church and others we know from our local community. What started out as a gathering of mainly young boys all squeezing together on the floor has turned into a gathering of lanky-limbed teens still trying to fit into the same small place.

While these get-togethers have often left our house in a fairly dishevelled state, these have been some of the best times of bringing people together (although the mood has on occasion been somewhat stilted if England played particularly poorly). Although there is no overt evangelistic agenda to this party, it has helped us to bridge the gulf between church and non-church friends, and over the 12 years that we have been doing this people have got to know one another and I have lost count of the times a friend has said to me, 'Oh, I saw that friend of yours from church in the supermarket last week and we had a good chat.' If we have homes and resources such that we can invite people over, then that is a great thing to do. And even if we don't, we can instigate a gathering of friends in a local park, a shared picnic or a walk together. We can be willing to go and visit others in their homes too, as we saw Jesus doing.

Jesus' prioritization of time with individuals in homes and in public challenges our tendency to think of evangelism as events that the church runs. Of course we must continue with such events, thinking creatively and strategically about how we can invite people into the life of the church, but the foundation must always be in personal relationships. As a church we need to be thinking much more about how we spend the 110 waking hours we *are not* in church than the two or three hours we *are* there.

Jesus also challenges us to consider *who* it is we spend time with. Jesus didn't confine himself to people of his own educational or working background. He spent time with the educated, the un-educated, the wealthy and the poor, men, women and children. One thing is for sure, we should never underestimate the radical nature of Jesus' ministry among women that we have recorded in the Gospels. He especially spent time with those who were overlooked and undervalued. When others tried to silence the cries of the blind man Bartimaeus, Jesus called him to him and healed him (Mark 10.46–52). When others were unafraid to ap-proach the demon-possessed man in the country of the Gerasenes, Jesus sets him free and restores him (Mark 5.1–20). When even his own disciples try to prevent the children from disturbing him, Jesus gathers them to him and teaches them about the kingdom (Mark 10.13–16). As always, Jesus is hard to pin down. Some of those relationships take place in the public sphere, in the religious gatherings, but the majority of them take place in shared commu-nity spaces or in the home. The challenge for many of us in the Church today starts with a willingness to get out of the safety of our church buildings and build friendships with the community around us.

Jesus related differently to different people

It is not just the fact of the breadth of relationships that Jesus had which is significant, but also the different ways in which he responded in each of those contexts. There does not seem to be a blueprint for how Jesus interacted with people. Each conversation is startlingly different.

In a fascinating article entitled 'Why Doesn't Jesus Preach the Gospel?', Pete Ward suggests that Jesus' approach in the gospel challenges our assumption in evangelism that the gospel is a particular form of words that needs to be expressed the same way each time. What we observe throughout the Gospels is that Jesus deals in a unique way with each person he meets. The things he says to the Samaritan woman, for example, differ from those he says to the rich young ruler or to the woman in the crowd who touches his cloak. Ward says this:

> Sometimes it is very difficult to reconcile the different things that Jesus says to different people. But what is very clear is that he varied his messages and actions to take account of the different people he met. In fact Jesus seems to be very much aware of what it meant to be poor, or powerful, or religious or a sinner, and he acts and speaks in the light of this knowledge. In short, the 'Gospel' as displayed in the ministry of Jesus, is not a static set of ideas but a relationship.[4]

That is not to say that becoming articulate in sharing the gospel briefly is not important. There have been times in conversation when someone has asked me what I believe and I have been glad of the ability to express it clearly and succinctly. There have been times on public transport or similar situations when I have not needed to deliberate over the words but have expressed clearly and without jargon why I believe Jesus is alive today. However, the greater skill is in the ability to integrate what we believe about Jesus with the reality of the person sitting before us, and this is where Jesus' approach can be helpful for us. Evangelism, then, views the person before us as a subject rather than an object in our conversation. Evangelism is not about communicating information but encountering the other. It is not something done *to* people but *with* them. Communicating as Jesus did requires us to give the other person our full attention.

Listen with an open heart not to judge but to support

When you read Jesus' encounters with people in the Gospels you get the impression that each person is held in his gaze. When the rich young ruler claims to have kept all the commandments, we are told that 'Jesus, looking at him, loved him' (Mark 10.21). In the midst of the bustling crowd, Jesus seeks out the woman who touched his cloak. In that moment, the needs of the wider crowd come second to Jesus' desire that this woman knows that she has been seen and that she is loved. There is in Jesus a relentless pursuit of the one over and above the crowd, and there is a personalized response given to each individual over and above a set formula or singular message.

Sometimes Jesus is the one who initiates the conversation. In the conversation with the Samaritan woman, for example, Jesus begins the conversation by asking her to give him a drink of water (John 4.7). In so doing, Jesus subverts the cultural norms of the day, but he does it in order to initiate conversation with her. Similarly with Zacchaeus, Jesus initiates the conversation. He senses Zacchaeus' interest (the fact he had climbed up a tree to get a better view was a bit of a giveaway), but Jesus is the one who calls him out of his hiding place and into hospitality (Luke 19.5).

At other times we see Jesus responding to the initiative of others. Jesus responds to the secretive but courageous action of the bleeding woman who reaches out to touch his cloak. Mark tells us that as she touched his cloak she was instantly healed. However, Jesus is not content to leave it at that, seeking her out in conversation so that she knows she is precious and loved (Mark 5.34). Jesus responds to the question of the rich young ruler (Matthew 19.16), the cries of the demon-possessed man (Mark 5.7) and the request by Jairus, the synagogue leader, to heal his daughter (Mark 5.24).

On other occasions, Jesus responds to the initiative of a third party. He strikes up conversation with Nathaniel, but only after Philip has introduced them (John 1.47). Jesus is able to operate in a different mode in each of these conversations, sometimes responsive and at other times taking the lead.

While Jesus deals differently with each of the people before him in such a way that it would be impossible to construct 'Jesus' seven-stage approach to evangelism', he does always seem to know what the next step each individual needs to make. In some instances, this next step is dramatic; for the rich young ruler the next step was to sell everything he had and give the money to the poor. But for the unnamed woman in the crowd, it was the knowledge of peace and reassurance. I have found it helpful to think in terms of 'steps' in my own encounters with people. It is rare to meet someone who is ready on the basis of one conversation with you to surrender their lives to Christ there and then. It can happen, but such instantly transformative encounters are few and far between. Thinking in terms of 'next steps' can be helpful and relieve the pressure. What is the one thing I can helpfully say to this person now that might help them to think Christianity is worth further exploration? What one comment might I make about Jesus that might make them intrigued to explore more about him? Viewing conversations in those terms can free us from either the paralysis of thinking we have to say everything and therefore saying nothing, or from saying too much and losing the person along the way. I like to imagine what it might take for someone to leave a conversation with me thinking, 'Huh, I've never thought that before.'

Jesus starts from a place of love

While Jesus might not appear to adopt a similar approach in the way he talks with people, there is one common thread that does run through his many encounters. Time and time again, Jesus begins the conversation from a place of love. In Matthew's Gospel we read about how Jesus viewed the crowd gathering around him. I have often wondered how Jesus coped with the constant demand for his attention, how he survived the pressure of people endlessly wanting to get something from him, and also how he balanced this alongside knowing he would then face criticism and even hostility from others as he did this. Matthew tells us that 'When he saw the crowds, he had compassion for them, because they were harassed and helpless, like sheep without a shepherd' (Matthew 9.36).

Jesus' starting point with people was from a place of love. The image of the shepherd would have been familiar to Matthew's readers who were steeped in the Old Testament Scriptures and they would have known it as an image used to describe the covenantal relationship between God and his people. The image of the shepherd in the Old Testament is also sometimes used to contrast with the ungodly leaders who are, in effect, *bad* shepherds (Ezekiel 34). Matthew tells us that Jesus is the good shepherd because he has *compassion* on his sheep. The phrase 'had compassion on them' carries a physical connotation, as though Jesus was moved 'in his gut' by the state of the crowds. And what is it that stirred this response in Jesus? On the one hand we might conclude that it is quite simple – people are in need. Jesus is constantly surrounded by those who are sick and in need of help. However, Matthew tells us that Jesus had compassion because 'they were harassed and helpless, like sheep without a shepherd'. Jesus is moved by the needs of the crowd but also by the fact that they do not realize who they belong to; they do not know who the shepherd is. They do not know the contentment and peace that comes from knowing that the Lord is their Shepherd. Psalm 23 is one of the most beautiful passages of Scripture and is one that I have spoken and even sung to my children during times of anxiety and uncertainty. The psalm speaks of a good Shepherd who watches over us all the days of our life, who is with us during the valley of the shadow of death. It is a psalm that essentially speaks of the promise of eternal life with a God who knows us and goes before us to conquer death. Jesus has this almost visceral reaction as he sees the crowd around them because he sees that they do not know God as their shepherd.

And our conversations too need to start from a position of love. Matthew 9.36 is a verse I have called to mind in a difficult conversation with someone or when someone has frustrated me, or pushed me, to recall how God views them. Remembering that God's heart is moved for each and every individual can help us in challenging or testing situations. It is a good discipline in our conversations with people to be silently praying, 'Lord, show this person that you love them and that you are their good shepherd.' This is the starting point to life in the kingdom of God.

Jesus' encounter with the Samaritan woman, which demonstrates his heart of love in evangelism, is one of my favourites. It is also the longest recorded conversation that Jesus has with any one individual in the Gospels (John 4.1–42). John tells us that Jesus and his disciples are travelling through the area of Samaria and that they stop in a town called Sychar (now the city of Nablus). John identifies Jesus' chosen resting place as Jacob's well. One cannot help but think back to the times in the Old Testament when wells were a place of meeting prior to betrothal. It was first at the well that Abraham met Rebekah and considered her a suitable bride for his beloved son Isaac (Genesis 24). Similarly, Moses met his wife Zipporah at a well (Exodus 2.11–21), and of course it was at a well that Jacob himself first laid eyes on his beautiful and beloved Rachel (Genesis 29). Is it not remarkable that it is by the side of the well that Jesus chooses to have this most profound encounter with a woman who we assume has deliberately chosen to come at a quieter time of day, away from the glare of other women, a woman with a complicated history of relationships and broken betrothals? And yet this is the very woman that Jesus seeks out to engage in the most profound (and very theological) conversation.

It is this woman to whom he offers the water of eternal life, this woman who leaves transformed by her encounter with Christ, and who, we learn later, becomes the first evangelist to the Samaritan people (John 4.39–42). As complex as this conversation is, its starting point at the side of a well is born out of love, a love that is more transformative than any love this woman has known previously. It is one of the most remarkable encounters, and challenges our perceptions about who God might raise up and call to be carriers of the good news.

Jesus made himself vulnerable

As we have already suggested, some of our negative perceptions about evangelism stem from a stereotype we have in our minds of someone who is sure of themselves, confident, able to answer every question and possibly a little arrogant to boot. One of the reasons many of us feel under-confident in evangelism is precisely because we don't think we have all the answers and we certainly don't want to come across as someone who is arrogant and aloof. This is one of the reasons why I love the way Jesus begins his conversation with the Samaritan woman: 'Will you give me a drink?' He begins by asking a question, by asking something of her. It is a humble and possibly quite vulnerable stance as Jesus expresses his need, in this case for a drink.

For several years I lived very close to a Kingdom Hall in South London and every week at roughly the same time a Jehovah's Witness would call at my door to engage in conversation with me. I was working from home and so the temptation not to answer the door was very real. However, keen to make the most of every opportunity that came my way, I would open the door and hear what the person had to say. I repeatedly found those conversations frustrating because it felt as though there was a formula they were following that allowed for no personal deviation. I didn't feel that those calling at my door wanted to hear what I had to say, they simply wanted to give me a copy of *The Watchtower*. When I replied, 'Thank you very much but I don't want a copy of *The Watchtower*, but I would love to have a conversation about who Jesus is,' they often started to retreat back down the garden path. I had clearly unsettled their planned objective.

All that changed once I made friends some years later with a lovely man named Yemi. When he passed me in the street one day he stopped to ask me this question: 'What do you think the future of the world is?' Because I guessed he might be a Jehovah's Witness and was pretty certain of the intention behind his question, I answered in a way that I probably would not normally to a stranger in the street and said, 'I believe the Lord Jesus Christ will return in all his glory and he will judge the living and the dead and we will all give an account for the way we have lived our lives.' Yemi was silent. He peered over the top of his glasses at me and I glimpsed a twinkle in his eye. We both laughed and this marked the most unusual beginning of a friendship I have ever had. Over the next few months Yemi became our friend and would even come and visit us with his wife and children, touchingly bringing us gifts at the birth of our third child. We once engaged in a Bible study together and were able to discuss honestly and respectfully our different perspectives on Jesus. Our friendship moved beyond just talking about our religious differences – in fact he was a follower of football and would often turn up on the doorstep just to chat about the weekend's football results. Moving beyond formula to genuine friendship in which you both give and receive is often the most fruitful place for the seeds of the gospel to take root.

When Jesus asked the Samaritan woman for a drink, he began the conversation with a posture of vulnerability. A common theme in recent thinking about mission has been the notion of 'receptivity' and the possibility of engaging in mission not as the one with all the power and all the answers but as one who has something to learn. Some of the worst examples of Christian mission in history have been based upon a kind of Western superiority that is far removed from the example of Jesus sitting by the side of the well in hot and dusty Samaria. It is interesting to note how frequently Jesus is the guest rather than the host. In fact we have no record of meals that take place at a home owned by Jesus; he is often reliant on the hospitality and provision of others. We tend to assume that hospitality is something we are to give rather than receive, but being those who are also willing to receive the hospitality of others means we relate to people from a place of vulnerability rather than one of power.

David Male and Paul Weston talk about this approach in terms of 'third-space evangelism' and suggest that historically our evangelism has been based either on a first-space approach – where we invite 'outsiders' into our territory to introduce them to Jesus – or a second-space approach were we go and engage in evangelism somewhere else (an overseas mission trip, for example). Instead they suggest the rather appealing idea of a third-space approach in which we journey with people to somewhere neither of us has been before.[5]

Earlier in this book I suggested that evangelism is invitational by nature but that it is based primarily on invitation to Jesus rather than to the Church. Our model for this is Philip who simply says to the sceptical Nathanael, 'Come and see.' Philip doesn't have all the answers to deal with Nathanael's questions about Jesus' origin but he can say, 'Come with me, and let's see together.' In essence this approach is a movement away from ourselves towards others, and then with those others to a place that is new for all of us. Our evangelistic conversations are not simply two-way, between us and our friend – Jesus is present in those conversations too, speaking to and with us both. The invitation is always away from ourselves and towards Jesus, towards an encounter in which we are both changed. 'Come and see.'

Jesus allowed himself to be interrupted

Prior to COVID-19 there were days when I would get up, look at my diary for the day and see that every single hour of the day was allocated to something: travel, work, meal with family, church meeting and so on. A thought would enter my head: 'I will get through today as long as I don't get any interruptions.' For so many of us with busy lives, crammed schedules and lists of priorities, interruptions are simply an inconvenience. The day will be successful if we don't have interruptions. However, Jesus' approach challenges us once again, since he frequently allows himself to be interrupted. One of the most significant of these interruptions is his encounter with the woman suffering from bleeding in Mark 5. Jesus is on his way to visit Jairus' daughter, a life-threatening situation with a huge amount of pressure for Jesus, not least on account of Jairus' high profile and reputation. In terms of priorities, I imagine Jairus would be pretty high on anybody's list. But in the crowd Jesus discerns the desperate plea of an unnamed woman trapped in sickness and misery and he allows his schedule to be interrupted, pausing not only to heal this woman but to engage her in a life-changing conversation. This delay, however, proves fatal for Jairus' daughter and Jesus finds himself subsequently faced with the need for a resurrection rather than a healing, and the unwelcome publicity that such a remarkable event naturally secured.

On another occasion, Jesus is teaching a large crowd who have gathered in a house in Capernaum. No doubt teaching was an important and strategic activity for Jesus' gospel ministry and yet along comes the interruption; this time suddenly and in the form of plaster falling from the roof and a paralysed man being lowered down on a stretcher. Jesus could have simply moved the crowd outside and continued his sermon there. However, Jesus allows the interruption, praising the faith of the four friends, and ensuring that the paralysed man is set free from both his physical ailments and his spiritual condition. Incidentally, this interruption turns out to be a remarkable opportunity in which Jesus teaches the crowd about his own identity; he is not merely a 'miracle worker' but the Son of God, who can offer what only God has the right to give: forgiveness (Mark 2.10). In fact when you read the account of this story, Jesus does not appear in the least bit perturbed by the friends' dramatic interruption; his frustration is for the so-called religious who allow their ideas of who God is and how he works to be limited.

I have found in my own life that the times that I have allowed myself to be interrupted by others have been some of the most significant times of conversation (although I have yet to be interrupted by someone breaking their way in through the roof). For example, there was a time recently when I invited a neighbour in who had been hoping to speak with my husband for medical advice but to whom I said that I had no medical knowledge but was happy to talk. This led to one of the most honest and vulnerable conversations we have had and one in which I was able to offer to pray, an offer that was received with gladness. As a result, my day started late and I was perhaps not as 'productive' as I had hoped, but I am pretty sure God was at work in the interruption. I find that beginning the day with the following prayer, 'God, open my eyes to see your interruptions into my day today' helps me to have the right attitude when those interruptions come and to remember that interruptions don't have to be inconveniences but can become God-given opportunities.

Jesus listened as well as spoke

Evangelism can be as much about not talking as it is about talking. What do I mean by that? Often our assumption is that in evangelism we need to tell people things. We have a message that we need to pass on and the most important thing is gaining a 'window of opportunity' in which we can share this. However, the more time I spend reading the Gospels the more struck I am by how varied Jesus' conversation is. Jesus, the one who really does have all the answers, spends a surprising amount of time listening and asking questions. Take, for example, the healing of blind Bartimaeus. Jesus and his disciples are heading out of the city with a large crowd gathering around them, and yet in the midst of all this noise and hubbub, Jesus manages to pick up the desperate cry of a blind man sitting by the roadside, presumably obscured from Jesus' sightline by the pressing crowd. Nevertheless, Jesus picks this one voice out of the crowd and gives him his full attention. It might seem a little strange that Jesus' first question to Bartimaeus is, 'What do you want me to do for you?' (Mark 10.51). We might think that it seems far too obvious a question for a mir-acle-worker to ask a blind man begging by the roadside. However, Jesus doesn't assume he knows what Bartimaeus wants. When Jesus asks the question he reassures Bartimaeus that he has been both seen and listened to. A similar approach is taken by Jesus when he encounters the crippled man by the pool at Bethesda and asks him, 'Do you want to be made well?' (John 5.6). Jesus does not presume to know what the man is thinking or experiencing in that moment, but asking the question enables him to hear and listen to the response.

Developing the skill of listening in evangelism enables us to get more quickly to the heart of the issue and to truly engage with the person in front of us. When our preparation for evangelism relies primarily on us learning particular outlines or set responses, there is a danger that these simply miss the mark when we are faced with the reality and complexity of this individual person.

As the writer of Proverbs puts it:

The purposes in the human mind are like deep water,
but the intelligent will draw them out.
(Proverbs 20.5)

'Intelligent' evangelism, then, is an approach that enables us to draw out what someone is really thinking and feeling. Listening allows us truly to understand a person and not just the 'stereotype' of that particular mindset. I get frustrated in conversations when people assume that because I am a Christian they automatically know what I think about certain things. We should guard against doing the same thing ourselves. I have many friends who are atheists and it would be easy to assume that they all have the same reasons for not believing in God, but I have discovered that the more I ask questions and truly listen the more I find their reasoning varies hugely, spanning from experiences of personal loss, to scientific objections, to personal upbringing and background. If I had never stopped to ask the question, 'Why don't you believe in God?' or, 'What has led you to your current position?' I would never have discovered this multitude of reasons. As with all relationships, listening is the key to going deeper.

Listening also enables us to discover the leaps that people need to make towards faith. For those of us who are from Christian backgrounds this is incredibly important because it can be really hard to imagine what it is like not believing in God. It is certainly nigh on impossible to put ourselves in the sort of position where we think believing in God is ludicrous or somehow even immoral. However, listening can take us a step closer to imagining what some of those obstacles and sticking points for people might be. It's healthy to put ourselves in situations where we are in the minority and where we feel out of our comfort zone; it can help us to imagine how people might feel turning up to church for the first time.

One day during Holy Week, my husband and I attended a communion service at St Paul's Cathedral in London. The service attracted a large number of tourists. I was sitting in an attitude of devotion as we were preparing to join the queue to receive communion. A couple of young female tourists were sitting behind us whispering rather loudly and as I prepared to stand I could hear their comments: 'Ugh,' one of them whispered rather loudly. 'Have you seen what they are doing? They're all drinking from the same cup.' 'Yuk, that's disgusting,' said the girl sitting next to her. For me, as someone who has attended church all her life and grew up hearing the story of the Last Supper and looking forward to being a teenager and being able to take communion for the first time, it struck me afresh just how peculiar some of our practices and assumptions look to an unchurched generation. It allowed me to see how much imagination is required by the Church if we are truly to 'put ourselves in the shoes' of those for whom the Christian faith is unknown and unfamiliar – and this comment was given by two girls who had at least had the courage and inclination to walk into a church service. And yet I was so thankful that I had had the privilege of eavesdropping, listening in on a conversation that pushed me out of my comfort zone, and gave me a deeper understanding of the growing gap between that which we in the Church assume is normal and the reality of people's experience outside the Church.

Jesus knew how to ask good questions

The way to develop this art of listening that we have been talking about is through simultaneously honing our ability to ask good questions. And of course Jesus is the master of asking brilliant questions. Did you know that in the New Testament Jesus himself is asked over 180 questions? But he directly answers fewer than ten of them. However, he does ask over 300 questions in return. It is our tendency to launch into little pre-prepared sermons that halt many potential evangelistic conversations. My experience has been that even when someone has asked me a difficult question, offering a question in response has been more fruitful in getting to the real heart of the issue.

Take, for example, the tricky question about suffering. Someone might ask us, 'How can a loving God allow suffering?' and our temptation might be to launch into a response, especially if we have thought about this question. We might want to talk about free will, human sinfulness and the difference between human-instigated and natural disasters. We might want to talk about the suffering of Jesus on the cross or point out that no religion has a perfect answer to the problem of suffering. There are lots and lots of different things we could say. In fact, Christian theologians have been debating this very question for over two millennia, so we could speak for an hour on the subject without drawing for breath. But how do we know which of these things to say? How do we know whether to say anything at all? And this is where asking questions and listening is so important. The person who is asking about suffering because they have recently lost a close relative does not necessarily need an academic answer about the free-will defence. In that moment they need to know that they have been listened to by you, and it may be appropriate to say something about God's promise to be with us in times of suffering or how you yourself have found your faith to help you in times of loss and bereavement. And so I have often found that when faced with a question about suffering I will tend to ask, 'Why do you ask that question?' or, 'What has led you to be concerned that God doesn't care about suffering?' On occasion, framing someone's question as 'Are you concerned that if God does exist that he doesn't care enough about our suffering to do something?' has led to a more poignant and personal conversation.

We would do well to spend time in the Gospels exploring Jesus' approach to people and how he uses questions, sometimes to unsettle but often to understand, to get to the heart of the matter. And just as we should not be afraid of asking questions, we should also welcome questions being asked of us. I would much rather get bombarded by questions I am not sure I know the answer to than be faced with a blank response of indifference. Jesus was not afraid of people's questions but sought to understand whether they came from a place of antagonism, doubt or personal pain. Developing the art of inquisitiveness will help us be better listeners and better question-askers, just as Jesus was.

Jesus' conversations were restorative and full of grace

The final challenge I want to draw from Jesus' encounters within the Gospels has to do with where his conversations with people end up. In the vast majority of conversations Jesus falls on the side of grace and acceptance rather than condemnation. He addresses the woman who is bleeding as 'daughter' (Mark 5.34). To someone who was considered ritually unclean and who had presumably not been touched in 12 years these words of Jesus were transformative. After his resurrection, Jesus seeks out Peter to reassure him that his denial on the eve of his crucifixion has not in any way lessened Jesus' love for him. To the man born blind he makes it crystal clear that his illness is not his fault (John 9.3). I remember once hearing a talk by a famous evangelist on how to disciple someone one to one. He was asked what the key was to making sure those new to faith became strong in their walk as Christians. I expected his answer to be reading Scripture and praying, arguably fundamental steps to effective discipleship, but he simply said, 'Grace, grace and then more grace'.

Jesus of course has words of judgement and condemnation also, but it is vital to note that his words of inclusion were often for those who considered they were excluded, and his words of exclusion were for those who presumed they were included. It is once again the topsy-turvy nature of the kingdom of God that subverts our ideas about who gets to be in or out. It is never our role as witnesses to judge others. It is not our place to convict them of their sin. To do so steps into the territory of the Holy Spirit. Our role as witnesses is to speak grace, grace and more grace. As disciples of Jesus we have experienced the love of God in Christ. It is our great privilege that we get to reveal this extraordinary love of God to people in ordinary ways, through everyday conversations, through listening and asking questions. In this way we are able to live his story: communicating not just what Jesus did but communicating like Jesus did.

For discussion

1 Taking your personality type into account, think of three natural ways you might share your faith. (These may not involve speaking explicitly of spiritual matters.)
2 Have you ever experienced an interruption that turned out to be a God moment? How might you become more prepared for interruptions in your everyday life?
3 What strikes you most about the way Jesus interacted with people? How might you learn from his approach?

5

Passing on the story of Jesus

How the Spirit guides us as we speak

All of them were filled with the Holy Spirit and began to
speak in other languages, as the Spirit gave them ability.
(Acts 2.4)

The Holy Spirit hit the Church at Pentecost like a dynamic explosion. This event happened at a strange sort of in-between time for
the disciples. Ecstatic to hear news of Jesus' resurrection from the
dead, their hearts had been filled with joy as they saw Jesus standing before them once again. A precious 40 days of meeting and
eating with Jesus again had turned them from the frightened individuals who fled at his crucifixion to courageous followers of the
one who had triumphed over the grave. But at Pentecost they find
themselves alone again. Jesus is no longer with them. However,
he has told them to stay in Jerusalem and wait for the gift of the
Holy Spirit. And then it comes. A sound like a rushing wind, which
reverberated around the place where they were gathered. Tongues
of fire appeared on their heads and they began to speak in languages
that were foreign to them: a familiar message in an unfamiliar
language. This is what they had been waiting for.

I can't help but imagine how this experience compared to what
the disciples thought might happen when God sent them his Holy
Spirit. Perhaps they thought it might be a quiet confidence that
filled them as they prayed. I suspect none imagined it would be
as explosive or dramatic as this – the extraordinary bursting into
the ordinary. As these miraculous events occur, a crowd gathers,
intrigued by what is taking place. Some of those gathered are trav-
ellers from as far away as Rome, and ask, 'Are not all these who

are speaking Galileans? And how is it that we hear, each of us, in our own native language?' (Acts 2.7–8). What is unintelligible to the disciples is accessible to tourists and pilgrims gathered in Jerusalem: an unfamiliar message heard in a familiar language. While some in the crowd began to mock the disciples, suggesting that they are drunk on wine, Luke is quick to point out that by the end of that evening, after Peter's sermon and impromptu baptism, some 3,000 were added to their number (Acts 2.41). That is a 2,500 per cent increase in church numbers for one day. As far as evangelism goes, this is pretty successful.

The Acts of the Holy Spirit

The dramatic way in which we are introduced to the Holy Spirit at the beginning of Acts demonstrates clearly the significance of the Spirit to the story that Luke is going to tell about these early years of the Church's life. The presence of the Holy Spirit bookends this fast-paced narrative, suggesting that he is its chief protagonist. Luke begins with Jesus' promise of the coming Spirit, swiftly followed up by the events of Pentecost itself. And the Spirit features significantly in Paul's final recorded speech at the end of Acts in which he makes a conclusive statement about his mission to the Gentiles (Acts 28.25). Through beginning and ending with the Spirit in this way, Luke is making clear that the primary witness to the events he is recording here is the Holy Spirit. The Spirit himself is the chief witness and agent in the mission of the Church. In fact, we might call this 'the Acts of the Holy Spirit' rather than the Acts of the Apostles. There can be a temptation to view the book of Acts as a guidebook for the Church, suggesting that we might find within its pages a blueprint for how to 'do' church. However, Acts is more concerned with telling us the story of how the first disciples witnessed to the risen Jesus in a world that did not know him. If that is the case then in our increasingly secular culture, which does not seem to know the God of the gospel, it has never been a more timely book. As we try to understand what beautiful and intelligent evangelism might look like in the twenty-first century, there is much we can learn from the first disciples in Acts.

The work and witness of the Spirit is integral to the book of Acts because the work and witness of the Spirit is integral to Christian mission and evangelism, and indeed the Church. The starting point of Pentecost begins as an outward explosion in Jerusalem, which ripples throughout the Middle East and eventually even further, fulfilling Jesus' promise that his disciples would be his witnesses in Jerusalem, Judea, Samaria . . . and even to the ends of the earth (Acts 1.8). Evangelism is impossible without the Holy Spirit.

As I was writing this chapter it rather coincidentally happened to be the week of Pentecost itself. However, this was right in the middle of lockdown in the UK and we were nine weeks into staying at home. It struck me with a sense of irony that I was writing about an outward explosive movement at a time when as a nation, and even as a global community, we were being compelled to stay inside. In lots of ways that felt frustrating to the mission and witness of the Church, as Thy Kingdom Come events and summer festivals were cancelled. However, I was also aware of research just starting to come out suggesting that people were encountering the Christian faith during the lockdown for the first time. I was also anecdotally hearing stories of God at work through this difficult time.

One afternoon, Sarah got in touch to tell how she had witnessed something extraordinary the previous day. Her church was involved in delivering food parcels to families who were struggling financially during the lockdown. Her job was to count the parcels into the car boots of the three volunteers who would then deliver these packages to families in need. She carefully counted the bags in and then counted again, getting her friend to check also, making doubly sure that the numbers were correct, and she duly sent the drivers on their way, praying that the families who needed them most would get help at this difficult time. Later that day all three drivers got in touch to say that when they had finished their deliveries the boot of their car still seemed to be full of food parcels and they were able to double back and give each family twice the amount of food than was originally intended. The families were overjoyed to see the drivers pulling up at the door for a second time. When Sarah spoke to me she was buzzing with enthusiasm at this modern-day feeding of the 5,000 and what she saw as an extravagant outpouring of God's love and the work of the Holy Spirit in a difficult time.

The Holy Spirit and evangelism

As the book of Acts clearly demonstrates, the Holy Spirit is integral to the work of evangelism. It appears that it is the Spirit who is influential in every key encounter or moment in the unfolding story of the Church in Acts, starting of course with Pentecost and the multiplication of the gospel into a myriad of languages and idioms. The disciples learned quickly that they were not in charge of God's mission, but instead they were being drawn by the God of mission himself. Their role was to follow where the Spirit was leading and to allow him to speak through them as they grew in boldness and courage.

Philip the evangelist – and the work of the Holy Spirit

One individual who follows where the Spirit leads is Philip. When persecution broke out we learn that while the Apostles stayed in Jerusalem, many of the early followers of Jesus were scattered but that 'those who were scattered went from place to place, proclaiming the word' (Acts 8.4). This is one of those examples where God is mysteriously still at work even through a terrible situation or crisis. I was interested to hear at an online event during the lockdown of one girl who had tuned into an online church service. She commented that she didn't go to church but her brother was involved in the service, and because she was missing him she tuned in to watch. This experience had her interested in the Christian faith, which she then wanted to explore. It is incredible how often God works through extraordinary or difficult situations, or times when our plans go awry, to bring new opportunities.

One of those who found themselves unintentionally scattered to Samaria was Philip, one of the seven who had been chosen to wait upon tables as the church started to grow. The Spirit prompts

Philip to go to the desert road to Gaza where he meets the Ethiopian eunuch. Luke tells us that this individual was a person of great influence, 'a court official of the Candace, queen of the Ethiopians, in charge of her entire treasury' (Acts 8.27). As Philip is told by the Spirit to travel alongside this man's chariot he heard him reading out loud (as would have been normal practice) a passage of Scripture from Isaiah. I suppose having a conversation with a stranger on public transport is the modern-day equivalent, although I have to say that in many years of such conversations, I have never met someone who 'just happened' to be reading Isaiah 53! Philip finds that the Spirit is at work in him enabling him to explain the Scriptures so that that this Ethiopian Chancellor of the Exchequer can hear and understand the good news of the risen Jesus. In fact the response is so immediate that the Ethiopian eunuch commands the chariot to be stopped so that he can be instantly baptized in a nearby pool of water. We don't hear of this man again, but Luke tells us that he 'went on his way rejoicing' (Acts 8.39) and we presume he then returned to Ethiopia as the first Christian disciple in that great continent of Africa. When we stumble across a chance conversation with someone on the train or the bus, we cannot know the impact our words may have or the seeds sown that will bear fruit in places and locations other than our own. Stories like Philip's should encourage us to seize every opportunity that comes our way and trust the Spirit to be at work.

God does not have favourites

The Holy Spirit is behind every significant and strategic moment in the mission and expansion of the Church in the book of Acts, constantly drawing the church into the fulfilment of Jesus' promise that they would be his witnesses in Judea, Samaria and to the ends of the earth (Acts 1.8). While we often think of Pentecost as a power encounter, it was also fundamentally a movement in accessibility: the barrier of language was removed as people were able to hear the good news of the risen Jesus in a way they could understand. This work of enabling people to encounter Jesus in a way they can understand seems to be indicative of the way the Spirit continues to work throughout the book of Acts, constantly propelling the first disciples out of their comfort zones to encounter people and communities, some of whom they suspected might be beyond the scope of the Spirit's work. We need this similar movement of the Spirit now to enable us to speak the good news of Jesus in a way people can understand and receive. It is the role of the Spirit in evangelism to keep us constantly looking for new places and people where the gospel needs to go.

One of the most remarkable of these Spirit-encounter moments is in Peter's meeting with Cornelius in Acts 10. At home praying one day, Peter receives a strange vision of a sheet containing some of the unclean animals that Jews were forbidden to eat. Three times Peter receives this vision and is told to 'Get up, Peter; kill and eat.' The message for Peter in this spirit-inspired dream is made clear: 'What God has made clean, you must not call profane' (10.15). Later that day, Peter has the opportunity to put this dream into practice when he finds himself at the house of Cornelius, a Gentile. Peter is quick to point out that it was not the done thing for him, a Jew, to find himself in the house of a Gentile, but he explains with remarkable clarity his own new thinking in this area: 'I truly understand that God shows no partiality' (10.34). I find it reassuring that Peter, who spent so much time close to Jesus, still had things he needed to learn. At this point in his journey, he still hadn't fully grasped that the good news was for all people and not just for people like him. As Peter shares the message with Cornelius and his family, the Holy Spirit begins to fall upon the Gentiles gathered, in similar ways to those experienced at Pentecost. And as the Spirit falls, those Jewish believers who travelled with Peter are 'astounded that the gift of the Holy Spirit had been poured out even on the Gentiles' (10.45). This is an extraordinary penny-dropping moment when the first believers grasp that the scope of the gospel is bigger than they had dared imagine, the love of God more extraordinary than they had thought, and that the missionary call upon them was far bolder and more extensive than they had realized.

It is hard to overstate the significance of this event, and the ripples that flowed out from it, eventually compelling the leaders at the Council of Jerusalem (Acts 15) to make the landmark decision that Gentiles did not need to be circumcised to be fully incorporated into the body of Christ, a decision that paved the way for Paul's focused ministry to take the good news to the Gentile world of Asia and Europe. It is worth pausing and reflecting for a moment that this historic shift in the church's understanding of the gospel starts with one individual's encounter with the Holy Spirit, which enables him to see and imagine how someone he previously assumed stood beyond the boundaries is actually welcomed in. All Peter and Philip do is simply follow where the Spirit is leading them. The first disciples are not in control of the mission of the Church: the Spirit is. And it is the Spirit who urges the Church on to new places, to new people and new locations, so that the gospel will go out to all nations.

Over the last few years, I have reflected at length on this story of Peter's encounter with Cornelius while I have taught on the subject of mission and evangelism to Church of England ordinands. It is so easy for our thinking in these areas to become limited, confined to what we know, what we are comfortable with and what we might consider possible. The story of Cornelius reminds us that the love of God and the reach of the gospel is always bigger than we imagine. In this encounter, the Spirit is at work not only in Cornelius and his family but in Peter also, enabling him to grasp that with God there are no favourites. I wonder who the 'Cornelius' in your life might be? The person whom you struggle to imagine could ever be a Christian? Perhaps it is an individual who seems too far away, too 'unchurchy' ever to find their way to church, or perhaps it is a whole group of people, perhaps those of another religion or a particular demographic of people that the church currently fails to connect with.

I am often tempted to feel overwhelmed when I think of my children growing up in such a secular world with so few Christian friends. The vast majority of those they hang round with at school have no connection with church at all and they often find themselves the only one in an RE class who might even be bold enough to say that they think Jesus was a real historical figure, never mind that he rose from the dead. However, if God goes to such extremes to draw Peter to Cornelius and his household, we must trust the same Spirit to be at work in reaching teenagers and young adults today in the secular West. Perhaps we are the ones, like Peter, who need to have our horizons expanded. We are the ones who need to be more imaginative and daring in the way we seek to engage such young people.

It is the Spirit of Pentecost that lies behind the gospel's expansion into the Gentile world, not the Church's clever strategizing or three-point vision plan, but the expansive, generous and pioneering work of the Spirit compelling the Church to engage with part of the world that it had thus far ignored or deemed beyond its reach. John Taylor was a missionary to Uganda in the 1940s. He served in Bishop Tucker theological college in Mukono, which is where my family and I spent three months in 2015. He described the work of the Spirit in mission in the following way:

> Mission is often described as if it were the planned extension of an old building. But in fact it has usually been more like an unexpected explosion . . . we should have had the modesty to recognize that the breath of God has always played a far more decisive part than our human strategy.[1]

For the Church in Acts this unexpected explosion of the Spirit among the Gentiles had some unexpected consequences that initially made things uncomfortable for the existing Church, compelling them to wrestle with big questions and change their way of doing things to welcome others. The Spirit propelled the Church out of its comfort zone to take risks and embrace the unfamiliar and the surprising, with no rule book to follow, and yet they embarked upon this adventure trusting that the Spirit was at work.

And so the question then remains for us: where is the Spirit drawing us today? Where is the new place, the new destination, to which we are being drawn in witness? Where is the Spirit already at work urging us to make the journey – literal or metaphorical – so that the gospel can find its way through us to the ends of the earth? What are the places in our culture where we imagine the gospel might not be able to find a home – the 'ends of the earth' kind of places on our doorstep? Where is God calling us to go? It might be to those in our own neighbourhoods whom we haven't yet truly noticed.

Good news and the place we find ourselves

From early 2020, the UK, like many other nations, began experiencing a tremendous upheaval as COVID-19 began ruthlessly to tear its way through people and communities. In the early days of the pandemic I lost track of the number of times the word 'unprecedented' was used by the media. Its frequent usage served to demonstrate that we felt unprepared for the wave that overtook us and the very unfamiliar territory of a global health pandemic. Had someone told me at the start of 2020 that I would spend four months locked down inside my own home with my children not attending school and GCSE exams not being sat, I would have shaken my head in disbelief. Overnight our congregations were forced to become familiar with video technology and social media as many clergy swiftly had to adapt to their new role as priest-cum-TV-presenter.

Tom Wright's book *God in the Pandemic* was published midway through the initial lockdown, helping us to sift our way through various Christian responses to the crisis.[2] One response I heard a lot was that this pandemic was a great opportunity for the gospel, as if to somehow suggest that God had engineered this to happen to enable more people to become Christians. I liked Tom Wright's comment that if we needed a global pandemic to make us realize evangelism was important then shame on us! However, as first-century disciples faced unwelcome persecution, twenty-first-century disciples have also faced an unwelcome situation, and we too have to find ways of sharing the good news in this strange and familiar context. It is not that this situation makes our sharing of the gospel more urgent; the urgency has always come from the nature of the gospel itself, as we saw Chapter 1. It is the task of all disciples to witness to the good news in whatever context we find ourselves. The context of a global pandemic is a strange and

arrogant

opportunity to spend time w/ Gospel & prayer

unfamiliar one for this current generation. We are surrounded by grief, and many of the inequalities that exist in our society have been brought uncomfortably into the light. In this unfamiliar place, the good news of the extraordinary love of God needs to be spoken with compassion, sensitivity and boldness by ordinary people who are living this situation too. The good news of Jesus has not suddenly become more powerful or relevant, but our sharing of it needs to become so.

What then can we learn from this book of first-century witness that might inspire us and help us as we navigate whatever the new normal might turn out to be? There are six principles that the first disciples discovered as they followed the guidance of the Holy Spirit, which can help us as we seek to reveal the extraordinary love of God in ordinary ways in the context in which we now find ourselves.

Risk-taking not comfort-seeking

What we learn from these first disciples is that the Holy Spirit is in the business of pushing people out of their comfort zone. It is the work of the Spirit that ultimately drives the church into new contexts that sometimes prove challenging. Peter took a risk in going to Cornelius's house. He took a risk that God had spoken to him through his bizarre dream, and the risk paid off and proved to be crucial for the future of the Church. In a great book called *Making New Disciples*, Mark Ireland and Mike Booker make the following pertinent comment on taking risks:

> We live in a risk-averse culture, yet there is something fundamentally risky about evangelism, when we are called to proclaim afresh the Christian faith in each generation. We learn by trying out new ideas, and finding out what works and what doesn't, and so perhaps 'success' in evangelism should be measured not in how many come to us, our courses and events, but how far we have been willing to go to reach the lonely, the lost and the broken with the good news of God's grace.[3]

The simple fact is that sometimes we will take a risk and it won't work out as we hoped. There have been times when I have taken a risk to invite someone to church or to an enquirer's event and they haven't accepted, but unless we take a risk we don't know. I remember once hearing Bishop Ric Thorpe (who is the Church of England bishop for church-planting) saying that we need more stories of failure. I was initially surprised by this but then understood what he was saying. If we don't have examples of where things haven't worked, then it probably means we haven't been taking enough risks. If we are to step outside our comfort zone, the chances are we will sometimes get it wrong or it won't work. Every time we step out of our comfort zone and ask someone if we can pray for them we take a risk, and in doing so we show our dependence on the Spirit because we cannot predict or anticipate the outcome.

When my friend Laura fell ill during the early days of COVID-19 she had the idea to record short video diaries of her experience of the virus and how her faith was helping her through illness and uncertainty. Though she had never done anything like this before, she took the risk of posting these videos on social media and found that friends and acquaintances who were not Christians started engaging with her about them. At the same time, as she convalesced at home, she noticed that each day people in her local area were walking past her house. Laura found a blackboard in the garage which she placed at the front of her driveway next to a basket that she filled with booklets about the Christian faith, with a note saying 'Please feel free to take one.' Each day Laura wrote a different message on the blackboard, often a verse from the Bible. During her convalescence she often saw people stopping to read the messages and then pick up a booklet, placing it in their pocket to read later. Even in a time of illness and uncertainty Laura had found a new way to share something of the good news with those in her local area. It was a risk but she was prepared to give it a go. Sometimes taking a risk can make us vulnerable, particularly if the response we get isn't great or if things don't go as we hoped, but it is often in taking the risk that we learn to rely on the Holy Spirit and allow him to work through us. We don't have to start with anything huge, but developing the habit of risk-taking is a great way to engage in creative evangelism. As those first disciples discovered, we too find that it is when we step out in faith that we are often surprised by the extraordinary things God does both in us and through us.

Variety, not one-size-fits-all

Our second principle is that the Spirit works in lots of different ways and it isn't easy to predict what the next move might be. While it is clearly possible to discern some core practices that the disciples engaged in, such as planting churches in the major cities of the region, the manner in which this happens is often hugely varied and highly unpredictable. At Pentecost, Spirit-led evangelism takes the form of public preaching. In Samaria it is a seemingly random conversation on a chariot. When we get to Philippi (in Acts 16), the church gets planted through a combination of exorcism, hymn singing and a jailbreak. It is hard to pin it down to one particular approach; the Spirit works in a myriad ways.

When it comes to the Spirit of God in evangelism there is no one-size-fits-all approach. The simple fact is we will limit our reach if we put all our eggs in one basket and invest in one form of out-reach. The way we will reach and connect with the elderly in our parishes will not be the same as the way we engage with teenagers or those in the workplace. Beautiful and imaginative evangelism requires us to be creative and flexible in order to reach all different kinds of people with the good news of Jesus.

This is one of the things that has excited me most about the emergence of the fresh expressions movement since the turn of the century, which has seen creative forms of church designed to reach and connect with different groups within our society. The Spirit of God is a creative and life-giving Spirit and we need this breath to permeate our minds as we seek to engage creatively with those around us.

Jane was involved in leading a Messy Church gathering once a month on a Saturday. One mum and dad attended regularly with their two children who enjoyed the craft activities and stories.

The mum was a committed Christian and regularly attended the Sunday service. However, her husband was not a believer and never attended church. Nevertheless, he enjoyed Messy Church and was happy to join in with the crafts, attending faithfully each month, and always sitting quietly at the back during the talk. Eventually Jane moved away to work for a different church but a couple of years later she returned and bumped into the mum of the family. The mum was keen to tell Jane that she was now studying theology and preparing to go into ministry full time. Jane asked how her husband felt about this life change and Jane was keen to tell her that he was now a believer and fully involved in their new church. She was keen to point out that Messy Church had marked a turning point in his life; he found it a safe place to be without being expected to get involved or know anything about the Christian faith. This had become a community through which he could eventually explore faith and come to know the love of God for himself.

Relational not confrontational

At the heart of the Spirit's approach to evangelism in Acts is the creation and formation of friendships, and often with unlikely people in unlikely places. I imagine that Philip did not expect to find himself in Samaria but he ends up staying there long term, living in a city on the coast called Caesarea where he spends his life in evangelistic ministry. Peter went on the roof to pray as was his custom but, as his stomach rumbles, he receives God's vision compelling him into a new set of friendships with those he least imagined. It is a recognized statistic that the most common way for someone to come to faith is simply through relationship. It seems to be the case that a cup of tea and conversation across the kitchen table is more effective than standing on a soap box at Speaker's Corner.

The gospel has always been shared from home to home, from person to person. It's just the way things are in the kingdom. The challenge is that many of us have relied on the Church to do the work of evangelism for us and have not seen the individual role that each one of us is called to play as witness in our everyday lives. While services and enquirers' courses can play an important part in someone's journey, they are not often the easiest starting point. We need to become better at starting the conversation with people across a coffee, while walking the dog in the park, while sitting in the waiting room. I heard recently of a journey to faith that started in a queue at a slimming group. These ordinary sites are often unnoticed places of Spirit-encounter. Ordinary human relationships can become the place where God's extraordinary love is poured out.

The question for us is, are we present in places where we might meet people who are searching and seeking? And are we ready to respond in love through word and action?

Seeing God not taking God

As we have seen in this chapter, it is the Spirit who plays the decisive role in the mission of the Church, taking the initiative and drawing the disciples into new contexts and places. The disciples' experience as they move into these new and different territories is that God is already at work; they are simply catching up with him. In the case of both the Ethiopian official and Cornelius, the disciples discover that the ground has already been tilled; all they have to do is sow the seed. Sometimes the thing that frightens us about evangelism is that we think we have to know all the answers. We assume that we have to see ourselves as the ones with everything to give, but the reality is that evangelism simply isn't like that. In fact, evangelism that barges in and assumes the Church has all the power and knowledge to bestow can do real harm. The problem with this perspective is that it puts the focus on us and what we have to bring and not on the person we are encountering and what God is already doing. The Spirit is always constantly going before us. It is not the case that we are taking God to places where he is not yet present; we are simply following where he leads and being invited to join in with what he is already doing.

One day my friend Kate asked me what to do about an experience her 8-year-old daughter had had the night before. My friend is not a Christian and is actually very sceptical about religion, but her daughter had recently become intrigued by the Christian faith. Kate told me that her daughter had woken her in the middle of the night to tell her that Jesus was standing at the end of her bed talking to her. My friend did not know what to do about this, and I could tell that she was quite concerned about this experience and how to convince her child this was a figment of her imagination. The first thing I enquired was whether her daughter had been frightened by this experience or whether it had made her feel safe. 'Oh,' Kate replied, 'it made her feel really safe.' 'Then there is nothing to worry about,' I reassured her. She looked at my quizzically and I said: 'Kate, I know you don't believe in God but just imagine for a minute that God does exist and that Jesus is his Son. It wouldn't be completely unthinkable, would it, for God to make himself known to someone and make them feel loved and safe?' Although Kate could not quite make sense of this experience she was prepared to imagine a different worldview in which this kind of experience could happen, and then became less confused and threatened by it. She returned home resolving to encourage her child in her desire to find out about God. In the same way as with my conversation with the hairdresser in Chapter 2, I found myself playing catch-up to the work of the Holy Spirit. I could never have engineered this conversation but my role as a witness was to put simple and reassuring words of explanation to what God was already doing. My job as a witness was not taking God into a situation where he wasn't present but simply seeing and responding to what he was already doing.

This means that in our everyday witness we need to adopt a posture of humility, recognizing that the results are not down to us and that we need to develop the ability to listen so we can sense and discern how God might already be at work.

There is a story in *Call the Midwife* where the sisters of Nonnatus House take a trip to the Outer Hebrides, which is talked about as Mother Mildred's mission from God. (It also conveniently provided some rather stunning scenery for the Christmas Day special!) Arriving on the Western Isles, the sisters are quick to get to work building a temporary clinic to provide for the expectant mothers in a place that has very little medical provision, and all appears to be going very well. However, as Christmas is approaching they start to decorate the local village hall with a Christmas tree and garlands, until a woman from the local community bursts in and accuses Mother Mildred of riding roughshod over their traditions and values. It would appear that putting up Christmas trees was something they considered offensive. In an uncharacteristic moment of sombre reflection, Mother Mildred utters these words: 'I fear I acted in haste and failed in humility in assuming that all the power to give and change and to illuminate was ours, or mine.'[4]

As we seek to live his story in our world today, we are not charged with the burden of taking God to places where he is not already present. Instead, we are called simply to listen and look for signs or openings where he might be at work and to ask him how we might join in. In so doing, we often find we are changed and shaped along the way. In the early stage of the lockdown, many of us felt as though our world had shrunk. As someone who is used to travelling for work and exploring different places, I suddenly found myself confined to what at times felt like a goldfish bowl of the same streets and places. And yet, as I took my daily exercise, pacing the same streets day after day, I began to notice things I have never seen before, houses I had simply rushed past. This season allowed me to walk more slowly, more intentionally, to look and to pray and to really notice things. How might you develop the habit of listening and seeing as you go about your daily life this Lent? How might you develop the skill of looking for the signs of God already at work, to which you can add your words and actions in witness?

Out there not in here

One of our faulty assumptions about evangelism is that ultimately it is about getting people 'in here' to our church buildings and services. Once I invited a local family to attend our Christmas carol service. They did not usually go to church but said they would like to come along. We met before the service and walked across to the church together, but as we reached the large wooden doors of the church their young child stood frozen to the spot. She grabbed her mother firmly by the hand and planted her feet resolutely on the ground. She was not going to walk into the church building. The mother found this hugely embarrassing and tried to cajole her child into church. I don't know what the child thought was going to happen to her if she walked through those doors but it was clearly not good and the whole family ended up leaving before they even got over the threshold. I popped round the next day to make sure they knew I was in no way offended by this, and we thankfully ended up laughing about it. However, if we assume evangelism is all about getting people into church, what do we do when people won't come? Or what do we do when people do come but don't like it? While few might react in such a physical way as this young girl did that December evening, many in our society today might have a similar feeling about church.

It is important that we think creatively about how we encourage people to come to church. While numbers of those seeking baptisms and weddings in church are decreasing, there are those for whom this still holds significance. Growing up in a vicarage I was aware of those who attended church when their children were about to turn school age, hoping that this might secure them a place in the local Church of England primary. While some attended for a short period of time and then left again, there were also those for whom this was the start of a renewed journey of faith.

However, in the book of Acts we discover that the disciples were often found 'out there' rather than 'in here'. Philip meets the Ethiopian on a public highway. Peter meets Cornelius at his house. In Athens Paul is to be found in the marketplace and in the meeting of the Areopagus (Acts 17.17, 22). In Ephesus we read that the synagogue turns Paul away, but instead he spends time teaching and discussing the faith in the lecture hall of Tyrannus (Acts 19.9).

Normal places at the heart of societal life quickly become places of Spirit-inspired encounters with the living Jesus. Ordinary run-of-the-mill places like markets and homes become sites of extraordinary encounter with the risen Jesus. The Holy Spirit transforms the people in those places, making us ask, 'Where then does God reside? In here or out there?' The answer is of course 'in both'. While inviting people to church will always be important, we need to remember that our mandate is also to go 'out there' and be present in communal spaces and communities. There are of course those who are housebound, who will never be able to attend 'in here'; there has always been the need to take the gospel into the homes of others, be that in person or online.

And so the question remains for us: where is the Spirit drawing us to today? Where is the new place, the new destination, to which we are being drawn in witness? Where is the Spirit already at work urging us to make the journey, be that literal or metaphorical, so that the gospel can find its way through us to the ends of the earth? What are the places in our culture in which we imagine the gospel might not be able to find a home – the 'ends of the earth' kind of places on our doorstep? Where are some of the forgotten people and places in our society that God might be calling us, like Philip and Peter, to open our eyes and see that 'God shows no partiality' (Acts 10.34) and that the ends of the earth have still to be reached.

Like many others, my church has found that running Alpha in a local pub has proved really successful. In our case that local pub was appropriately named 'The Hope Pub' but I'm sure 'The Coach and Horses' could work equally well. I was interested to hear during an online Alpha course I was involved in during the lockdown, one person commenting, 'I would never have gone on an Alpha weekend away in person, but here in my home I feel safe to explore.' Getting out of the place where we feel safe (our church buildings) can often involve being in a place where others feel safe.

This perspective can transform the way we view our workplaces. If markets and riversides can become places of missional opportunity, then so can our workplaces. Many of the people we work with live too far away from our churches to attend, but the workplace itself can be the place of 'out there' witness.

My friend Liz works for a large accounting firm and one Holy Week she took some hot cross buns into work and left them in the communal kitchen. She then sent an email around to everyone in her department saying that they were probably aware that she was a Christian and so Holy Week was an important time for her as she reflected on Jesus' death. She said that she wanted to share this special time with her colleagues and so had left the hot cross buns as a treat for people to enjoy in the break times. She also signed off by saying that if anyone wanted to talk with her about what her Christian faith meant to her she was really happy to chat. Liz received a positive response, with lots of her colleagues replying to her email saying they appreciated the gesture and others stopping by her desk to talk with her. Such initiatives do not have to be huge but when we start to view our workplace as an 'out there' place of missional encounter we can open the door for witnessing.

One of the features of the Church's response to the COVID-19 global pandemic has been the revelation of this tension between 'in here' and 'out there'. For a season the possibility of being 'in here' was denied, at least in terms of physical buildings, and the Church has had to seek new and unfamiliar ways of being 'out there' online, resulting on occasion in some hilarious mishaps of dogs interrupting live streams of the Eucharist and one poor vicar who accidentally set himself on fire during Evening Prayer. However, this global pandemic, as terrifying and serious as it has been, has not been the first that the Church has faced in its history and will not be the last. Rodney Stark is a sociologist who has studied the origins of the Church and sought to explain how and why the Church grew so extensively in the first few centuries. One of the observations he makes in *The Rise of Christianity* is that when epidemics came, as they frequently did, the wealthy pagans would flee to the hills for safety, but the Church would stay, caring for the sick, witnessing through terrible times, sometimes even at the cost of their own lives.[5] The Church, through such pandemics, was shown to be reliable, compassionate, unafraid to run towards the crisis rather than away. The Church was determined to be 'out there' as a witness.

Claire lives in a cul-de-sac in a small town in the Midlands that is not far from the local church where she works. On the first week of the lockdown, Archbishop Justin suggested lighting a candle at

7 p.m. on Sunday evening as part of a national call to prayer. Claire sent a text to the messaging group of her cul-de-sac saying that she was going to be doing this and if anyone had any particular names they wanted her to include then to let her know. Another woman in the group suggested that they should light the candle together on the street and offered a large candle for this purpose. So, at 7 o'clock that Sunday evening Claire ventured outdoors to light her candle with her neighbour and saw that five other families had also gathered there – two metres apart, of course. Claire found herself having to come up with a little impromptu sermon about light in the darkness, and they lit the candle and said a simple prayer. The woman who had brought the candle with her suggested that they should do this again the next week. This gathering continued throughout the 16 weeks of the lockdown and is still happening now. Claire has become very adept at preparing a short thought from Scripture each week to accompany this action. On each occasion, a different number of families and individuals turn up, the vast majority of whom have never attended church, yet find this simple act of lighting a candle and saying a prayer has helped them through a difficult time. Claire's boldness in being 'out there' has enabled her to reveal something of the extraordinary love of God to people right on her doorstep.

Together not alone

The final principle that we can draw from the experience of the disciples in Acts is this: 'together not alone'. We can often presume that evangelism is a solitary activity and this can lead us to feeling lonely and unsupported as we seek to witness to those around us. However, once again the book of Acts seems to tell a slightly different story. The disciples were rarely on their own as they sought to proclaim the good news of Jesus to people. When Peter visited Cornelius's house he took some of the other disciples with him, even though visiting a Gentile's home was not really the done thing. Reading through the ends of Paul's letters is great for getting a sense of the partnership that Paul enjoyed as he travelled to new and different places.

Partnership with others

Witnessing was never meant to be a solitary activity but something we do together in partnership with others. This is not only because it is easier that way but because it can also be more effective. The whole church community has an important role to play in evangelism. It is increasingly the case in our culture that people are looking for a community they can belong to before they are looking for something they can believe in. Sometimes they simply need to belong, and belief comes later. I remember being on an enquirers' course when one man said the reason that he had decided to come was because of cooking! I asked him to explain more and he spoke of how his wife was a Christian and attended the local church, although he himself was not a believer. He told me that when they had had their first child the church brought an array of home cooking each night to support them through those first couple of weeks of sleepless nights and exhaustion. The community in action had clearly moved him, and was part of the reason why he wanted to explore the Christian faith for himself.

Lesslie Newbigin was a missionary in India (from 1940 to 1970) and when he returned to the UK in the 1970s he was staggered by the cultural change that had taken place during that time, in particular the emergence of other religions and how the Church was declining from the centre of society's life. He spent the rest of his life wrestling with this changing culture and what it might mean for the proclamation of the gospel. He repeatedly grappled with the question, 'How might the West be converted again?' I had the privilege of meeting him once not long before he died when I was a university student. His sharpness of mind, coupled with gentleness and humility, had a big impact on me. While Newbigin suggests many responses to his question, the one that lies at the heart of his thinking and is perhaps best known is his statement that 'the church is the hermeneutic of the gospel'. What Newbigin meant by this was that as the West becomes increasingly secularized, people might no longer pick up the Bible and read it but they might see the message of the Bible lived out in the Christian community. People are more likely to be attracted by a community that authentically lives out the good news of the kingdom in the world around them. The message of the gospel might be something that is seen in practice before it is understood.

My friend Damien, who now works as a civil servant, came to faith at university. He was not brought up as a Christian; his home environment was anti-religious, although his grandparents did occasionally take him to church where he helped to hand out the hymn books. In his final year at university Damien became aware that he was not happy with his life. He was achieving everything he had hoped and dreamed for but something didn't quite seem right and he became more and more unhappy. Plucking up the courage to ask a girl he liked out on a date he was met with the response, 'You can take me to church if you like,' and so he tentatively agreed to go. There Damien found a community of people he was drawn to. He recalls that there was something about these new friends that he found highly appealing. They seemed to him to have something that was genuine and true. He described it to me in the words, 'It was as if I had been living in the night when they lived in the day.' Over time Damien started to explore the Christian faith and found answers to some of his previous scepticism, but his starting point had been being drawn and attracted to a community of people who welcomed him and made him feel there was a place where he could belong and be himself. This safe place then provided the foundation from which he could enquire and explore and eventually meet Jesus for himself.

Partnership with God

However, it is not only partnership with other Christians that challenges our notion of evangelism as a solitary activity. Evangelism is only effective when done in partnership with the Holy Spirit. The disciples become witnesses to the ends of the earth because the Spirit is given to them (Acts 1.8). The book of Acts shows how they follow the lead of the Spirit. This can be a tricky tension to get our heads around because if it is ultimately the Spirit at work then why do we also need to go? However, it is the Spirit who enables all disciples to live out their calling to be witnesses. As Jesus promised his disciples, it was when the Spirit came that they would know what to say (Luke 12.12). The Holy Spirit enables us to be who we are called to be as witnesses to the risen Jesus. And the Spirit will also use our words and actions to open the eyes of the blind and set the captives free. We are never alone but always work in partnership with the one who can bring new life in places of darkness and death. This means that evangelism is simultaneously not at all about us and also very much about us.

Luke makes clear at the beginning of Acts that the way that Jesus will be with us as we seek to make disciples is by his Spirit, given at Pentecost and repeatedly poured out on those who have followed this Jesus ever since. The Spirit of Jesus is the Spirit of witness who is constantly at work in and through the disciples. Luke ends the book of Acts in an open-ended way. It is not the dramatic finale you might expect from a book that is so jam-packed with drama and adventure. I have a feeling that was entirely deliberate on Luke's behalf, making clear that the work of the Spirit is not yet done.

What now?

One day during our time in Uganda we visited the village of Kayunga where a great pastor and pioneer of the faith called Titus had lived and planted a church. The current church pastor, Felix, was eager to show us the gravestone of this faithful man of God, which was behind the church building. The gravestone was nothing impressive to look at, embedded in the ground, simple and rough, with a thin layer of orange dust covering the top, beneath which these words were roughly inscribed:

> *I have fought the good fight, I have kept the faith,*
> *I have finished the race.*
> *HOW ABOUT YOU?*

The book of Acts ends with that self-same question for us: how about you? How about me? The Holy Spirit continues to be at work today, still seeking to use us in remarkable and surprising ways, pushing us out of our comfort zone to glimpse the ways that he is at work so we might join in with him. Where are you prepared to go? Will you join in?

For discussion

1 This chapter encourages us to think globally. How can you perceive the Holy Spirit at work during the COVID-19 pandemic?
2 The Spirit often 'propels us out of our comfort zones'. Have you ever surprised yourself by speaking boldly, or can you think of someone else doing this with remarkable results?
3 The work of the Holy Spirit is mysterious . . . Can you think of a situation which has been transformed beyond imagining by the work of the Holy Spirit?

6

Finding echoes of the story of Jesus in our world today

Building a bridge to the good news through books and films

'As I went through the city and looked carefully at the objects of your worship, I found among them an altar with the inscription, "To an unknown god." What therefore you worship as unknown, this I proclaim to you.'
(Acts 17.23)

I love giving presents. I think it's possibly more exciting than receiving them myself (although I also like that!): the sense of anticipation (mingled with a tiny bit of fear) when you offer something to someone and hope they will love it. I remember one birthday morning handing my son Jesse, then four years old, a very obviously wrapped football for him to hold it in his hands and say rather optimistically, 'Maybe it's a toy train?' I realized at that moment I had not been listening as well as I should have been to what was top of the list that year. By contrast, my father-in-law is an exceptional present buyer. Every year at Christmas, I am struck by the thoughtfulness of his gifts and how well-suited they are to my children. The individual nature of his choices reveals that in those precious moments, when the kids sidle up to him on the sofa and chat about their favourite footballer or pop band, he has been listening, mentally taking note and remembering it months later. Unfortunately, I have told him I think he is an excellent present buyer and he says this has now unduly put him under pressure. The gift that means the most is not one that is most expensive or the biggest under the tree, but the one that has been bought with you especially in mind. What lingers in our heart is that another person stood in a shop or at a craft stall at the market and thought of us and what might make our face light up. Gifts, even small and inexpensive ones, can be powerful demonstrations of how well we are known and loved.

Knowing where to begin

The gospel of Jesus Christ is the greatest gift we could ever offer to another person. To share with another human being the good news that in Christ we are known, loved, forgiven and set free is truly the greatest gift we could give them. But as with other gifts, we need to be thoughtful in how we offer it, giving consideration to what and how we might best connect God's story to the person in view. There is so much we could say about the good news and its themes of love, redemption, reconciliation and God's grace. One of the greatest challenges we face is in knowing where and how to begin the conversation.

Steve Hollinghurst uses the analogy of a packet of seeds, which is helpful in exploring how we might develop the art of knowing where to begin our conversations.[1] Hollinghurst suggests that instead of viewing the gospel as one single seed, which when planted produces a single plant, we view it as a packet of seeds, which, when sown together, produce a whole garden of beautiful flowers. As sowers of the gospel our first task is to discern which seed to begin with so that in time we might sow the whole packet of seeds. This kind of approach requires us therefore to develop the skill of listening, ensuring that our evangelism relates to where people are at and the questions they are really asking, rather than communicating a formulaic message that fails to connect.

Paul in Athens

One of the best examples of this thoughtful gift-giving approach is seen in Paul's visit to Athens in Acts 17. He shows us an example of intelligent and imaginative evangelism. Athens was a famous location in the first-century world. Boasting a strong intellectual heritage from the Greek philosophers of the fourth and fifth centuries BC (the likes of Plato, Aristotle and Socrates), its incorporation into the Roman Empire had not dampened its reputation as a city of immense intellectual and educational importance. Paul had grown up in the city of Tarsus, which was also well known as a centre of philosophy and a plethora of Hellenistic religious cults. While Paul was steeped in the Scriptures as a Pharisee, his background in philosophy meant he was well prepared for his missionary trip to Athens.

As was his usual custom, Paul goes to the central meeting places of this historic and busy city. He speaks the good news of Jesus in the synagogue but also in the marketplace. It is not long before Paul is creating a stir and arousing the interest of the philosophers of the day. In particular Luke mentions the Epicureans and the Stoics, who gathered around to hear him speak and to debate his ideas. The Epicureans were agnostic secularists; they were not concerned about the possibility of gods, as they considered them too far removed to be relevant to human life even if they were real. The Stoics, on the other hand, were pantheists who believed in a strong sense of unity between humanity and the divine. To the Stoics, God is everything and everything is God. While these two types of philosophers were very different from one another, Paul's preaching about the good news, and in particular the idea of resurrection, clearly aroused a response. Whether they wanted to argue against him and disprove his new and unfamiliar teaching or whether they were intrigued by the possibility of Paul's new teaching, they all wanted to hear more and so brought him to the Areopagus, a place where the latest ideas were discussed and debated. Despite the apparent pluralism of Athens, Paul's teaching about Jesus and the resurrection caused a stir and people were intrigued. Paul had a captive audience of philosophers and the latest thinkers of the day when he addressed the crowd.

However, before looking at Paul's approach in Athens, it is worth noting how Paul initially felt when he arrived in this strange and unfamiliar place that had not yet heard the good news of Jesus. Luke tells us early on that Paul 'was deeply distressed to see that the city was full of idols' (Acts 17.16). A more literal translation of Paul's deep distress might be that 'Paul's spirit was pained within him'. Just the sight of this huge city bursting to the brim with idols to various different gods caused a visceral response for Paul the evangelist. His belief in the uniqueness of Jesus as the way to the Father stood in stark contrast to the religious world view in front of him. Gone is the hot-headed Saul who would have his way through coercion and control, as we see at the beginning of Acts. Instead we see a different Paul, still as passionate and zealous but now resolute to show that the deepest desires of the Athenians can only be adequately met by the risen Jesus. Paul is determined to show this with wisdom, grace and clarity. In so doing, he provides us with an effective model for how we can present the gift of the gospel in such a way that it relates to people's deepest longings and connects with the culture around us. The gospel cannot be delivered in a vacuum but is always spoken in a particular language, clothed in particular phrases and concepts. Paul's model shows us how to do that in the different situations in which we find ourselves, especially those where the message of the gospel seems peculiar or even alien to the surrounding culture. What we see in Acts 17 is imaginative evangelism at its very best.

Step 1: Looking and listening

Our tendency is often to assume that evangelism always begins with talking. However listening is frequently a better starting point. Just as teaching a small child to cross the road involves looking and listening in order to prevent many a dangerous disaster, so looking and listening in evangelism can save us many a disastrous encounter. As we have seen, Paul's first move in the strange and unfamiliar city was to look and listen. He spent time walking around the city, observing what was going on. This means that later on he was able to make reference to one of the altars he has observed and he was able to quote their own poets to them. Paul spent time looking and listening so that he could better understand the people to whom he is so eager to present the good news of Jesus.

Our first step, then, in seeking to engage in imaginative

evangelism is to become skilled observers and listeners. We need to hone our ability to notice what is going on around us and to understand what it says about what other people cherish as most important in life. I am always fascinated by the bestseller lists because they serve as cultural barometers, showing what is currently capturing people's attention and interest. I often read a book that is repeatedly on the bestseller list even if it isn't one I would naturally choose, simply to understand what all the fuss is about.

It can be tempting to regard the time that we spend watching TV or films as primarily time to switch off from the realities of our everyday lives. Media can become a form of escapism in which we retreat from the world. However, a survey conducted by *The Independent* in 2018 suggested that the average Briton spends around 27 hours a week watching television.[2] And during the lockdown, TV viewing increased significantly.[3] While we all need time to 'switch off' and rest, we can still be inquisitive about the things that we watch and read. Here are some simple questions I try to ask myself about popular things that I observe, to help me become better at looking and listening:

- What does this book/film say about what human beings are like? Are they good? Flawed? Both?
- What ideas does this book/film have about what are the most important things in life?
- What does this book/film say about God or any ultimate meaning to life?
- What problems in the world does this film reveal, and what is the cause of them?
- Who is the hero or heroine, and why? Who is the 'villain', and why?
- How does this film suggest you might find meaning in life?
- What does this film say about the future of the world and our role or God's role in it?

It is unlikely that any film addresses all those questions and it may only focus on one. But those questions help us get beyond the 'Did you like the film?' response and on to the deeper questions about worldview and meaning. In this way, we ensure that as disciples of Jesus we do not retreat from the world, but, like Paul in Athens, learn to look and listen so we might be more effective communicators of the love of God.

Step 2: Giving credit where credit is due

Paul may be 'distressed' by the idols that he sees around him but he begins his speech on a positive note of affirmation. 'I see how extremely religious you are in every way,' he says (Acts 17.22). This is not a mere platitude to win people over, but a genuine acknowledgement of what is positive in the Athenians' experience. In so doing, Paul positions himself as a fellow religious seeker. He has established bonds of trust and openness right from the start. Paul may have become accustomed to explaining the Old Testament in the synagogue, but on Mars Hill he knows making reference to the history of Israel will not connect. Paul appeals instead to the book of nature and the idea of God as Creator. He picks up on the intuitive sense that the Athenians had that God was present, and he uses this as his launch pad to speak about the good news of Jesus.

Alister McGrath suggests that the idea of 'clues' can be useful in this imaginative approach to evangelism:

> God's existence may not be proved, in the hard rationalist sense of the word. Yet it can be affirmed with complete sincerity that belief in God is eminently reasonable and makes more sense of what we see in the world, discern in history, and experience in life than its alternatives.[4]

What we are aiming to do is to identify the 'clues' in the world around us which point towards the gospel, or provide a foundation upon which a conversation can be built. Such clues might be the inherent value of human beings, the beauty of the created world, a hunger for justice or a desire for hope. Each of these are clues that point towards the good news of Jesus and ultimately only find their fulfilment there. However, when we spot them in books, films, pieces of art, we can affirm their goodness and value. They can be the first stepping stone in a conversation, or a foundation on which we can agree. Paul's opening comment that the Athenians were 'very religious' was an affirmation of their hunger for spirituality and ultimately their search for God. Paul saw this and, rather than being dismayed by the object of their religious devotion, he begins by crediting them for their desire for devotion in the first place.

One of the 'bestselling' books of 2018, which I purchased purely to see what all the fuss was about, was Jordan Peterson's *12 rules for Life*.[5] While there was much about his approach that I strongly disagreed with, the fact that this book had sat atop the bestsellers' list for so many weeks was intriguing. In our secular culture where we are told people do not want definitive answers or grand metanarratives for life, where religion is seen as restrictive of one's life choices, here was a book strangely advocating 'rules' for life. I was curious. Peterson does not claim to be a Christian; in fact he somewhat confusingly calls Christianity 'a true myth', but he frequently uses Christian concepts and Scripture in his writing. Peterson suggests that where religion used to provide culture with a way of finding meaning in the face of the bewildering uncertainty of the world around us, secularism has created a void of meaning which needs to be filled. He suggests that it is possible to find such meaning once again and that it will be found by the pursuit of goodness. His 12 rules indicate 12 ways you can structure your life in the pursuit of meaning in the chaos. It is hard not to see a parallel between this and a Palestinian preacher who stood on a hillside 2,000 years ago offering eight very different 'rules' for life. However, regardless of my personal opinion of Peterson's 12 rules, the popularity of his approach revealed something important about people's hunger for meaning and where they might seek to find it. I can't help but imagine that if Paul had been wandering into Waterstones in 2018 he would have been quick to affirm people's hunger for meaning in the chaos of secular life. In my own experience, reading Peterson's book opened up interesting and significant conversations with non-church friends who were drawn to his approach. A hunger for meaning and order was a good foundation from which to begin a conversation.

Step 3: Looking from a different angle

The third step in Paul's approach is that he invites those listening to look at life from a different angle. Paul takes what was familiar to them and that which he could affirm, in the Athenians case their inherent religiosity and appetite for meaning and truth, but invites them to look from a slightly different perspective. He acknowledges their search for God, demonstrated through the idols and altars, but he also shows where that worldview ultimately falls short. He notes that they have an inscription to the unknown God and uses this as a starting point to talk about a God who does not dwell in shrines made by human hands. He expands the vista before them to see the true God that their spiritual longings point towards. He talks about the living God who has revealed himself.

Paul's approach here is both affirming and confrontational. What was a monument to polytheism, Paul turns to a discussion about the one true God. He finds the fault line in their worldview (the altar to an unknown god was possibly there to ensure that all divine bases were covered) but he uses it to talk to them about a God who has made himself known. That which they cannot put a name to, he will identify and speak about. On the one hand Paul dismantles their worldview, yet he does it in a manner that points to the way in which God lies beyond their spiritual searching; the fulfilment of all they have been searching for. In continuing to engage relevantly and sensitively with the Athenians, Paul uses quotations from their own poets, but he shows them in a fresh light.

Tim Keller uses the phrase 'subversive fulfilment' to describe the kind of approach we see Paul adopting.[6] There are also echoes here of the way Jesus engaged with the Samaritan woman. In talking about the Samaritan woman's pursuit of love, Jesus points to a deeper love and fulfilment that can only be found in relationship with him. In effect, Jesus says to her that what she is looking for is found in him, but also that he is so vastly different from what she thinks she needs. In Athens, Paul adopts a similar approach. He suggests that the Christian God might be the 'unknown god' that they are seeking. However, he also talks about how this God is not like any of their other gods since he is the one who made the heavens and the earth. He builds on the foundation that is already there – but he expands it and blows the perspective wide open.

When we watch a film or read a book, we need to be looking for deeper questions that are raised, upon which we can build a conversation. What are the foundations we can say 'yes' to and affirm, but can also say 'and yet . . .' and point to more? One example of this would be the hugely popular musical film *La La Land*. On the one hand it has the classic feel of a Hollywood love story; Mia, a girl with a dream of being a Hollywood film star meets and falls in love with a Jazz pianist, Sebastian. However, this love story is far from simple and the narrative becomes focused on the choices they make in life and whether pursuit of one's calling is more important than pursuit of love or even happiness. Sebastian's criticism of LA culture is that it 'worships everything but loves nothing'. The film raises the question, 'What are we to do if love stands in the way of the thing we were called to do or the person we are called to be?'

If we were to adopt Paul's approach to this film there is a lot we can affirm as a foundation: the film recognizes the uniqueness of each individual and the freedom each person has to make choices. It affirms our capacity to dream and long for a better future. However, the film also shows the impact of pursuing our own dreams, perhaps at the expense of others. *La La Land* raises the question of how we make the 'right' choices in our life. What do we do when those choices don't work out the way we intended or when others let us down? Is there an overarching narrative to human life or are we purely autonomous individuals who can create our own destiny? By asking questions about the 'message' of the film we begin to discern the worldview behind it. Once we start to understand what the film thinks is most important in life, then we are able to enter into conversations about ultimate meaning and purpose.

Step 4: Pointing to Christ

The final stage in Paul's approach in Athens is to point people to Jesus. As we have seen, Paul uses the altar to an unknown god to affirm the spiritual nature of the Athenians and challenge their belief in gods who live in shrines. In this final stage, Paul clearly explains who that unknown god is and calls the people to repentance and faith in the risen Jesus.

Paul points out that they have been looking in the wrong place for religious fulfilment and have instead worshipped idols made by human hands and not the living God. He uses this exposition of their worldview to show them their need for repentance, but he reassures them that they can put their trust in the one who stands between life and death. This is the Easter story brought alive once again, this time on a hot and dusty hillside in Greece. Jesus is the only one who has been raised from the dead. Paul ends his speech on a triumphant note of Christ's uniqueness and saving power, and urges those listening to put their trust in him.

It can be all too easy in conversation never to get round to the Jesus bit. We can enter into deep conversations about the meaning of life but unless we point people to Jesus we are not fulfilling our calling to be witnesses to the risen Lord. Paul, in Athens, does not say everything he could about Jesus. You only have to read his letters to see just how much he possibly could have said, but he simply points to the uniqueness of Jesus and our need of him.

I was once in a taxi being taken to a conference centre where I was due to be speaking to clergy in the Chelmsford Diocese on the subject of evangelism. It was not hard to get into a conversation with the taxi driver about faith because he asked me what I was going to be doing at the conference. This particular taxi driver liked to talk and was keen to tell me all about the faith he didn't have and his firm belief that all religions were ultimately the same and the cause of all the evil in the world. I had the opportunity to share with him a little of what I believed, to which he responded with the phrase, 'I don't mean to offend you, but what you believe is a complete load of rubbish' (only he didn't use the word rubbish). As we pulled up to the conference centre the taxi driver kept talking and talking, telling me how much he really didn't believe in Christianity. I couldn't stop him talking and was, somewhat ironically, almost late for my teaching session on evangelism. At the end of our conversation I said some final words to him that I often say in this kind of conversation. I simply said, 'There are lots of reasons why I am a Christian but the most important of these is that I am simply irresistibly drawn to the person of Jesus. I am drawn by who he was, the things he said and did and the fact that he rose from the dead. That's why I am a follower of Jesus.' At this point I thanked the guy for driving me, paid my fare and motioned to get out of the taxi. The taxi driver said, 'What time do you need a ride back to the station? I'll come and pick you up. I'd like to talk more then.'

The gospel as a story

When Paul wandered around Athens he was trying to understand the story of the culture he was in. Paul knew how to explain the story of the Christian gospel from start to finish, but he knew that in order to connect with those around him he needed to understand their story and relate it to the things that they knew and understood. As a narrative, the Christian gospel addresses four important questions that lie at the heart of human experience. Beautiful and imaginative evangelism requires us to hone our ability to see echoes of these questions in the world around us.

Who are we? What does it mean to be human? What is the purpose of human life?

Creation tells us that we are made in the image of God, valued, loved and capable of doing good and looking after the world around us. The biblical understanding of human anthropology is that we are freely capable of loving and being loved and can know God.

What is wrong? What is the problem with humanity? How do we account for sin, evil and injustice in the world and in ourselves?

The Fall tells us that humanity also has a propensity towards wrongdoing and evil. Our tendency to put ourselves in God's place has disastrous consequences for our relationship with the world, people around us, ourselves and ultimately with God.

What's the solution? What has God done about this situation? How has God acted in the world to put things right?

God has intervened in the world through the sending of his only Son Jesus. These are the events we reflect upon during Lent and celebrate in Holy Week. In Christ, God takes on human flesh and walks among us. His life, death and resurrection are the means by which our relationship with God is restored. We call this salvation. The Bible uses a variety of different images to explain how God puts things right. There is the image of sacrifice in which Jesus stands in our place. There is the image of the law court in which Jesus pays the price for our sin, which we ourselves should pay. There is the image of the estranged son who is welcomed home by the grieving father. The image of adoption is also used to describe the way in which God loves us and chooses us to be in his family. The Holy Spirit is given to us as a sign and seal of our adoption. In fact, salvation is so rich a concept in the Bible that it cannot be confined to one image alone. Reconciliation, adoption, sacrifice and redemption – they all teach us something about how God has intervened to rescue humanity.

What's the future? Where is human life heading? Is there life beyond death or is this all there is? What does the future hold for us?

Jesus speaks of eternal life that begins now. In Christ we are offered life in abundance; it begins now and lasts for ever. God is restoring the whole of creation and bringing in all things under the feet of Jesus. As disciples of Christ we enter into the new life in the kingdom and live by the fruit and gifts of the Spirit as we witness to the good news.

Of course, there is far more that can be said about what the gospel is and all the many ways that Scripture explains and points to this narrative. However, simplifying it into these four core questions can provide us with a way to develop the kind of approach that we see Paul engaged in in Athens. It is rare in conversation that we get the opportunity to explain the gospel from start to finish. However, it is quite likely that we can become engaged in a conversation that addresses one of these four questions. They are so fundamental to the nature of human existence that it is not surprising that they frequently surface in films, books and TV programmes. If the gospel of Jesus Christ is the defining story at the heart of the universe then we should expect other stories to point towards it. Learning to spot these four questions in films and books can lead to conversations that go deeper and engage with some of the bigger issues of life. Such conversations can become beautiful and imaginative places of witness.

Two recent productions have more obviously brought up Christianity as a topic of conversation. The first of these is the *Two Popes*, a delightfully written film exploring the imagined friendship between Pope Benedict XVI and Pope Francis. It is moving in its exploration of forgiveness and unity and makes for a fascinating conversation starter. The second is *Messiah*, which centres on a somewhat enigmatic figure who appears in the Middle East accompanied by peculiar manifestations such as freakish weather, rumours of healing and even walking on water. The CIA suspect he is a charlatan or even an unknown terrorist. But others flock to him, presuming he is the second Messiah. It is an intriguing film for exploring how people might have responded to Jesus in Palestine 2,000 years ago and for asking questions about the possibility of the miraculous and how we might respond if such a figure were to appear. These kinds of films resonate overtly with Christian themes, and questions such as 'Did you see?' and 'What did you think its main message was?' open up conversations that can dig a little deeper than questions of personal preference and taste. However, any film can relate to one of the four gospel questions. Once we become attuned to look for them, they can act as a springboard to deeper conversations that ultimately point to the story of the gospel. Here are some examples of recent films, books or TV programmes that engage with these four questions.

Question 1: Who are we?

The Most Human Human is another one of those books that I wouldn't normally read but an agnostic friend recommended it to me as something he would like to talk about with me and so I jumped at the chance.[7] *The Most Human Human* is an auto-biographical account of Brian Christian's experience of taking part in the annual Turing Test, which is a competition designed to pit the most advanced artificial intelligence (AI) software against a human being. A panel of judges fires questions ranging from moral dilemmas to celebrity knowledge and questions about personal preference at the hidden contestants. The judges then have to decide which contestant was 'the most human human'. Brian Christian's book narrates his experience of not only participating in this competition but his year-long preparation in advance of it.

Through his research Christian offers fascinating commentary on the increasingly sophisticated 'chatbots' that we encounter in everyday life. Such AI systems excel in a test such as the Turing Test on account of their ability to think digitally and break down information into small separate chunks. If human beings have been understood as unique on the basis of their ability to reason and synthesise various fragments of information, and this is now something a computer can do faster and more effectively, in what way can we talk about the uniqueness of being human? Brian Christian, however, is not just a computer scientist, he is also a phi-losopher and a poet and it was these aspects of his understanding that enabled him to win a decisive victory in the Loebner Prize. Christian discovered that where the computers excelled in process-ing information, he was most convincing through his use of poetry and human language and particularly poetry's reliance upon allusion and context. In addition it was in the unpredictability and spontaneity of some of his answers that his humanness became most apparent. *The Most Human Human* seeks to respond to those most crucial questions, 'Who am I?' and 'What does it mean to be human?' As I suspected, reading this book enabled me to have a really interesting conversation with my agnostic friend about what is unique about humanity and what I as a Christian thought it meant to be made in the image of God.

As we have already seen, *La La Land* also seeks to answer this question about human identity and the consequences of our free choices. Even programmes such as *Love Island* ask questions about what defines us as human beings and whether appearance and sexual relationships are to be the defining factors in our lives. Such films and programmes can raise important questions not only about the nature of human existence but also its purpose.

Another book that addresses the 'Who am I?" question is *Machines Like Me* by Ian McEwan,[8] although this book takes a slightly darker turn and begins also to engage with our second question, 'What is the problem with the world?' Brilliantly written and superbly observed, *Machines Like Me* has an Orwellian twist in that it imagines a parallel world to our own – an alternative take on the 1980s in which the UK has lost the Falklands War and Alan Turing is alive, having devoted his life to the development of AI. A bachelor named Charlie Friend spends his family inheritance purchasing one of these synthetic humans, interestingly called Adam and Eve. With his love interest, Miranda (a sure reference to the character Miranda in *The Tempest* who cries, 'O brave new world'), a younger woman lodging in the flat below, they together programme 'Adam' according to their own interests and preferences, and so their journey begins and their lives become inextricably tangled around Adam's presence. As the novel develops you discover that several of these Adams and Eves have chosen to end their own existence, having failed to come to terms with the realities and inconsistencies of human existence.

I thought it would be a novel about love and perhaps raise the inevitable question, already imagined in the film *Her*, is a robot capable of love? But the novel largely focuses on the idea of truth. Is the robot capable of keeping a lie? Is the thing that marks humans out as distinctive not merely our capacity to love but our ability to deceive, even those we claim to love? This took me back to the first session of an online Alpha course I ran at the beginning of the lockdown when, in response to the opening question, 'If God were real what question would you ask him?', one young woman simply said, 'Why do we do bad things?' A Christian understanding of self explains that we are capable of both goodness and evil, of both truth and deception, of beauty and ugliness. After all, in the garden of Eden, the place in which human beings were both the recipients and givers of love, it is deception that soon follows the fall of humanity. As Adam and Eve try to hide themselves from God, Adam is quick to try to deceive God into thinking that his companion is purely to blame: 'The woman whom you gave to be with me, she gave me fruit from the tree, and I ate' (Genesis 3.12). It would seem that the capacity both to love and to deceive are profoundly and inescapably part of human experience. And so it is remarkable that McEwan's robot, also named Adam, seems to some degree capable of love but incapable of deception, and it is this which more frequently creates the conflict with his human 'owners'.

In asking the simple question, 'Who are we?' or 'What does this book/film say about what it is to be human?' we are not far away from the core questions of the gospel and that which is both so troubling and so intriguing about the human condition. The Christian gospel has the answer for why and how we are capable of both truthfulness and deception, goodness and evil.

There have of course been times in the history of the Church when the tendency has been to emphasize one aspect of our human condition over the other. We can probably all think of times when evangelism has felt so 'heavy on the sin' that we were uncomfortable, but a gospel without reference to sin cannot possibly be good news to human beings who are capable of both truthfulness and deception, goodness and evil. In my experience, finding places in literature where both of these aspects of the human condition are in evidence has been a great starting point for that troubling question, 'Why do we do bad things?' and leads naturally on to the subject of how Jesus understood these dual aspects of our humanity.

For example, in Jesus' encounter with the woman at dinner at Simon the Pharisee's house in Luke 7, Jesus acknowledges both of these aspects of this woman's humanity. While she wept at his feet as she anointed them with perfume, Jesus praises her for her generosity and humility, particularly in contrast to the absence of any hospitality from his host who should have known better (Luke 7.44). However, he also acknowledges her many mistakes through his parable about people in debt. His words, 'Your sins are forgiven', speak not only of this woman's sinfulness but also of the possibility of her restoration. The unique truth of the Christian gospel is that we are more sinful than we realize but more loved than we ever dared imagine.

One of the challenges we face in evangelism is that when confronted with their own sinfulness people have too often felt that the Church is precisely not the place for them. However, in the Gospels it is precisely to Jesus that the sinners run. He is the one with whom they feel safe and accepted and begin to imagine the new possibilities of a transformed life. When I was ordained at St Paul's Cathedral I invited a friend to attend the service. She was delighted but looked a bit surprised. 'I've never been to church before. Are you sure it is all right?' she asked. I reassured her that of course she would be welcome and I would be honoured to have her there. I then asked why she thought she wouldn't be welcome. 'Oh,' she replied, as if this was the most obvious answer in the world, 'I didn't think I was good enough.' Responses like this make me want to weep. How have we allowed ourselves to give the impression that we are better than everyone else? How have we allowed ourselves to give the impression that Jesus' words 'your sins are forgiven' are for others before they are for us. Conversations about the Christian understanding of anthropology and what it is to be human can become the doorway to removing some of these misconceptions, bringing us to the heart of the gospel, both in terms of what it says about us and where it points us – to Jesus. This conversation with my friend about the Church is one of many times in which I have found myself changed and challenged through the experience of sharing my faith, times in which I have found myself having not only something to teach but something to learn.

Question 2: What's wrong?

There is an abundance of films that address the question, 'What is the problem with the world?' After all, the premise of human sinfulness often makes for riveting viewing material. There are two recent productions in particular that seem designed to make us question our deeper motivations in life and open our eyes to our own lack of integrity. The first of these is the powerful yet darkly satirical South Korean film *Parasite*. This enthralling film is a modern-day parable, narrating the stories of two very different families: the poverty-stricken Kim family, whom we see living in a dingy and grimy basement, straining to use the Wi-Fi of the premises above and building pizza boxes for a living, and the wealthy Park family who live in luxury yet are beset with anxieties about the behaviour of their young, spirited son. The film revolves around how their lives become entangled with one another through a web of lies and deceit. What starts as a clever deception as the Kim family daughter gains lucrative employment by posing as a qualified art therapist to help the Park's young son, eventually securing a faux job for each member of her family, spirals out of control with horrendous consequences. The film is a modern-day parable of the consequences of lies and deceit. However, while the Kim family are clearly the ones who lie and deceive, the Park family soon reveal that wealth cannot cover over their hypocrisy and prejudice. The film suggests that we all have secrets buried away that we are not prepared to be revealed. 'Parasite' raises questions not only about the wrong choices we might make in life, but also how we all have prejudices or a hidden side that we try to conceal.

A similar approach is taken in the recent Netflix series *Little Fires Everywhere*, based on the book of that name by Celeste Ng. Ostensibly it is a drama about racial tension set in the idyllic town of 'Shaker Heights' in Cleveland, Ohio. The first episode begins with the dramatic burning down of a large family house, and the following eight episodes fill in the causes that led up to that event and reveal that even those who consider themselves to be 'good' and 'unprejudiced', when put under pressure, reveal hidden ugliness and their very worst traits. It is a great series for talking about the secrets that we hide and the less than glamorous truths about who we really are.

As we have seen, one of the biggest challenges we face in our evangelism is around the concept of sin. It is a term that many people struggle to connect with, often either associating sin with the stringent 'forbiddens' of a bygone religious ethic, or else trivializing and talking of it as an indulgence. There is a brightly coloured sweet shop in Covent Garden in London called 'SugarSin', which illustrates this perfectly. However, the gospel makes little sense to people unless they know their need of God and in particular their need for forgiveness. It is not our place to force people into feeling guilty. It is the Holy Spirit who will convict the world of sin (John 16.8). However, engaging in conversations where we are forced to peer into some of the hidden corners of our lives can be an important starting point for some. On a recent enquirers' course I was interested to hear that one of the women attending had come because she had recently taken part in an AA programme. The 12 steps begin with the acknowledgement that the person is helpless in the face of their addiction and that he or she needs a higher power to overcome it. The woman attending said she had come to find out more about the higher power who had helped her with her addiction. It struck me that beginning an exploration of faith with that recognition of need of a higher power was a really good place to begin and I was thrilled that this woman was wanting to know more about the 'unknown god' who had helped her.

Question 3: What's the solution?

One does not have to look far to find films that focus on the idea of rescue and redemption as their central narrative. The themes of adoption, reconciliation, redemption and substitution form the core plot of many films and books that entertain and enthral us. Even some of our favourite children's films centre on this premise. In *Frozen*, Anna sacrifices herself to save her sister Elsa. 'You sacrificed yourself for me?' Elsa asks. 'I love you,' came the reply.

Toy Story 4 is another heart-warming film that explores the notion of love as having redemptive value. Forky is a rather peculiar-looking toy made out of rubbish by a little girl who wanted a friend. Surrounded by other strange-looking toys who have been rejected because they either don't work or are no longer in fashion, Forky suffers from self-rejection and keeps wandering off and throwing himself into the garbage. What starts out as humorous actually becomes rather poignant as he repeatedly says, 'I am trash.' Forky's story takes on a new direction once he realizes that he was made for a purpose and loved by the one who made him.

The theme of sacrificing oneself for the life of another is a common theme in films that draw us in. In *Infinity War*, one of the most significant films in the Marvel Avenger series, Thanos is seeking the infinity stones, six elemental crystals that each control one essential aspect of human existence. Thanos, the powerful super-villain, manages to obtain three of these stones because someone was in each case willing to surrender them in order to save the life of another. It appears that one individual's life is more precious and valuable than the cosmic battle. *The Hunger Games* series are similarly good for watching with teenagers and exploring themes of good and evil and the role of self-sacrifice.

Other films deal more seriously with the themes of rescue and redemption. *A Bridge of Spies* is based upon a true story from the 1950s during the Cold War. A somewhat nervous lawyer, played by Tom Hanks, is given the task of representing a Soviet spy who has been captured on US soil. It is an incredibly moving story, demonstrating that every life matters, even the so-called guilty ones. The tense and moving finale on the bridge in the dead of night involves the idea of one life given in exchange for another.

Les Misérables is a classic story that has had various incarnations based on the nineteenth-century novel by Victor Hugo. It tells of the Frenchman Jean Valjean who is released from prison after serving 19 years for stealing a loaf of bread. However, it appears that he can never escape his past record until a priest shows kindness to him and he starts to get his life back on track. It is a gripping story and hence famous for a reason, but the gospel themes of forgiveness, justice, mercy and grace reverberate strongly through the film.

Question 4: What's the future?

The question of life after death has recently been most overtly addressed in the Netflix series *The Good Place*. Eleanor Shellstrop, a typical party girl with a self-obsessed lifestyle and a fair amount of engagement with low-level crime, dies unexpectedly after a collision with a bunch of shopping trolleys (it is a rather quirky series). She wakes up surprised to find herself in the idyllic bliss of the Good Place, where she can choose her own frozen yoghurt flavours and a house has been made just for her. She is even more surprised that evening when Michael, the architect of the Good Place, superbly played by Ted Danson, informs the group of newly arrived residents that a cosmic mathematical calculation has weighed their good deeds against the bad and that they just tipped the scales and made it into the Good Place. At this point, Eleanor realizes something must have gone wrong in the eternal moral calculation and knows that she should really be in the bad place. She decides simply to keep quiet and enjoy her newfound eternal life. This works until events start to go wrong around her (in the form of giant prawns and a swarm of bees that mess up the perfect Good Place) and it becomes obvious that her presence in the Good Place has upset the eternal equilibrium.

Without wanting to spoil the story, it becomes obvious that nothing is quite as it seems and that the route to eternal life is more complex than a simple evaluation of good and bad. As the series evolves, the character of Chidi becomes important, a moral philosopher who helps people better themselves. In fact this becomes the key to achieving any hope of the eternal bliss with which the Good Place began. One further theme becomes apparent as the five series unfold – that of the concept of time. As people better themselves, 'passing' various moral tasks or tests of their character, the idea of perfection, even the perfect relationship, becomes interminably boring. Even Jason, the hilarious DJ from Florida who is obsessed by a particular computer game, discovers that when he reaches the top level there is nothing more for him to seek or achieve. Eternal nothingness then seems the only logical option.

The Good Place is a fascinating and hilarious commentary on

133

different perceptions of the afterlife, beginning in the first series with a more traditional idea of good being weighed against bad, raising the question, 'What is good enough, and do any of us make it?', through to the final series' comment on the monotony of the eternal. It is a comedic reflection upon the impossibility of a timeless eternity without a divine being. At one point we are introduced to a figure who is called 'the judge' but she is as fickle and uncaring as the rest of them, certainly not a being to be worshipped. Heaven as simply a continuation of the best possible moments on earth ultimately becomes its own form of hell. Heaven without God is ultimately meaningless.

Looking for the questions

Learning to identify these four questions in films, TV series and books are just some of the ways in which we can build a bridge from the subjects that engage and entertain people to the good news of Jesus. For many people today, their lack of interest in the Christian faith is not because they consider it intellectually flawed but more commonly because they do not see its relevance. It just doesn't seem to engage with the kind of issues and questions that people are interested in. The burden upon us as witnesses of the gospel is not to prove the truth of the gospel but to demonstrate its relevance to people. Developing an approach like the one I have outlined here is just one way we can foster deeper-level conversations with friends, neighbours and colleagues. It doesn't have to be about films or books. The same can apply to art, music, sport or anything that people are interested in.

In Athens, Paul sought to connect the good news of Jesus with the world around him. He engaged in imaginative evangelism. He sought to build bridges between people's current experience and his claim that Jesus, the judge of the world, is risen from the dead. There has never been a more urgent time for us to deploy this kind of creativity and responsiveness in our evangelism, since we find ourselves in a culture that has largely forgotten its need of God and in which the Christian narrative holds little or no relevance for people. The world around us is full of 'clues' that point to the gospel story at the heart of the universe. Our task as witnesses is to look for those clues in everyday life and draw attention to them, arousing curiosity and intrigue in conversations. We need to develop the art of seeing what is already there, becoming good interpreters of our culture so that through it we can point to the story of the gospel and what Jesus could mean to those we meet and talk with.

Preparing for the response

When Paul finished his speech in Athens with his grand finale of the resurrected Jesus, he faced three kinds of responses (Acts 17.32–34). There were those who mocked him and thought he was out of his mind. I suspect they might have used the Greek equivalent of the 'rubbish' word. The second category of people are those who wanted to hear more on another day. However, there is a final group who that day became followers of Jesus. Like Paul, we too will face those three different responses. There will be those who think that what we have to say is 'rubbish'. However, Paul does not force it upon them. Instead he moves on. In evangelism we need to learn when we have said enough. We are to use persuasive and creative ways to share this good news with people but at the end of the day it is an invitation that can be accepted or rejected. Jesus is looking for those who will open their hands and receive the gift. It is never ours to wrestle or force into someone's grip. However, there will also be those for whom an initial conversation sparks an interest. They aren't ready there and then to follow Jesus but they want to hear more. With these people we need to be more persistent and intentional, seeking out other conversations with them, perhaps offering them something to read. Then there will be those who are ready to follow Jesus, and we need to help them take those initial steps along the pathway to faith. It is on these first steps that we will focus in the final chapter.

For discussion

1 Which book or film that you have recently absorbed might give you a way of sharing the gospel – or more generally talking about the big questions of life – with others?

2 Do you regularly check out some of the things causing a stir in popular culture and, if not, how might you (enjoyably!) keep yourself well informed?

3 In what book, film, drama, musical, TV programme or radio broadcast do you find a winning presentation of the gospel?

Stories of finding Jesus

Understanding the different
ways people come to faith

> 'Whether quickly or not, I pray to God that not only you but also all who are listening to me today might become such as I am – except for these chains.'
> (Acts 26.29)

In my second year at university I lived in a shared house with nine other students. It was chaotic and noisy but a lot of fun. During this year I was involved in organizing a mission week with the Christian Union called 'Choose Life' at which Michael Green spoke every evening on the subject of the gospel. I invited each of my housemates to attend one of these events with me and, even though I was the only one involved in the Christian Union, most of them agreed to come. One of my closest friends in the house was a guy named Chris. Chris had been brought up in a nominally Roman Catholic home but by the time he arrived at university he was pretty sceptical about religion and would probably have called himself an agnostic. Nevertheless, he agreed to come to one of these talks with me. He was interested by what the speaker had to say and so agreed to come back again another night to discuss further. Chris was studying law and enjoyed debating with me and frequently presented me with counter objections to the Christian faith and questions that I often couldn't answer. After the second of these evening talks, Chris and I stayed up late into the night, sharing drinks on the grungy student sofa, talking about the Christian faith. We discussed science, evolution, heaven and hell and Jesus' crucifixion. In the early hours of the morning Chris made it clear to me that I was never going to convince him and he didn't want to explore the Christian faith further. I felt bitterly disappointed but knew I should respect his wishes. I went to bed with a heavy heart that night.

We continued to be friends throughout the rest of our time at university but the conversations about the Christian faith largely stopped. After university Chris moved up north to work as a lawyer, I moved to London and we sadly lost touch. Fifteen years after leaving university I received a message from Chris on social media, saying he had been trying to get in touch with me again. He proceeded to tell me how, when he had left university, he became an aggressive atheist. At this point I started to doubt my effectiveness as a witness. Had sharing a house with me for two years driven a mildly sceptical agnostic to full-blown atheism? Am I that terrible at evangelism? He then proceeded to tell me that a few years later he had met a lovely woman and got married and started a family. His wife was keen to get the children christened in the local Church of England church and he had agreed to go along with this. At this local church he encountered such a warm welcome, which he described to me as follows:

> I felt a tangible spiritual reawakening, like an old friend had returned to me with his arms open. It was quite remarkable. I instantly recalled our chats and finally understood what you meant. My journey started with you, Hannah, and I'm pleased to say that your faith and guidance paid off in the end. I've been eager to get back in touch ever since.

Blinking away the tears I too recalled the conversations and how futile some of them seemed at the time. I remembered the disappointment I felt in the early hours of that morning and my heart began to burst with joy. How little we realize the impact of our words upon people. How long the journey towards faith can be for people. How patient and prayerful we must be.

Long or short

The book of Acts records for us many of the conversations the Apostle Paul had with those who were sceptical about the

Christian faith. One such conversation came after he had spent two years imprisoned on a false charge, when Paul finds himself before King Agrippa in Acts 26. Agrippa stood in the lineage of a string of kings who had opposed truth and righteousness, not least Herod the Great who had tried to kill Jesus as a young child. And now Paul himself stands before the King, seeking his help and ultimately awaiting his fate.

Paul's response in this situation was, as on numerous occasions, simply to tell the story of God's work in his life. He does not engage in legal argument about his unlawful imprisonment but honestly and openly traces his journey of faith, from his religious childhood, through the dramatic encounter with the risen Jesus on the road to Damascus, through to his present situation. The only defence he needs is to narrate his experience of God's work in his life and he does this calmly and full of respect for his listeners.

What is particularly striking in this testimony is the boldness with which Paul directs his question to the King himself: 'King Agrippa, Do you believe the prophets? I know that you believe.' One can imagine the shock at the brazenness of Paul's question to the King, demonstrating that all those years in prison have in no way dampened his courage. The King's reply is similarly feisty, questioning Paul: 'Are you so quickly persuading me to become a Christian?' Suddenly the attention is not upon Paul's story but on the King's reaction to it. It is evident that Paul's testimony leaves the 'what about you?' question lingering in the air. Paul's response reveals a profound truth about the ways in which people come to faith: 'Whether quickly or not, I pray to God that not only you but also all who are listening to me today might become such as I am – except for these chains' (Acts 26.27–29). In this statement Paul reveals his evangelist's heart. The beauty of Paul's evangelistic approach in this incident is the transparency of his desire that every person listening would meet Jesus. However, his use of the phrase 'quickly or not', translated in the NIV as 'long or short', indicated what Paul had learned about the variety of ways in which different people made the journey of faith. For some, their experience would be an instant moment of conversion, a crisis point in which their life is instantly changed, but for others it would take more time, a slowly evolving movement towards faith in Christ. What may appear as a somewhat throwaway comment from Paul is actually a principle that gives hope to us as we seek to witness to those around us. Since receiving the message from my friend Chris, this idea of 'long or short' has been both helpful and hopeful in understanding that the journey towards faith will look very different from one person to another.

Two different roads

One way in which we can think of this difference is in terms of two roads: the road to Damascus and the road to Emmaus.

Paul's experience on the road to Damascus is a dramatic account of personal conversion. This is the story Paul chooses to share with Agrippa, drawing a stark contrast between his previous and his present life (helpfully in this case indicated by two different names, Saul and Paul). In Paul's case it was one dramatic encounter with Christ that led to a complete turnaround in thinking and action. Some of you will identify with Paul's story and will be able to pinpoint the precise moment in your life when you became a Christian.

However, there is also the road to Emmaus. Remember the story of the disciples walking along the road soon after Jesus has risen from the dead? They are discussing the rumour of resurrection, trying to make sense of the enormity of what has been claimed. Suddenly a stranger starts walking alongside them, asking questions of them and talking about the Scriptures. Intrigued by this man, and it being late in the day, they beg him to stay with them. And at the evening meal, as this oddly familiar man breaks bread, the penny drops and the two disciples realize that this stranger is the risen Jesus (Luke 24.31). When Jesus disappears again, the two disciples reflect upon the day that had passed: 'Were not our hearts burning within us while he was talking to us on the road while he was opening the Scriptures to us?' (Luke 24.32) Looking back on their journey, they realize that he was there all along; they just didn't see him. They recognize that what they experienced as hunger and desire was actually the presence of Christ with them, already drawing them in; it was only later that they realized who he was. The road to Emmaus can be a picture of a slower, more gradual journey to faith, less dramatic but equally authentic, and it resonates with many of us.

The reality is that a lot of people's faith experience is more Emmaus than Damascus, a gradual process often involving many influences, people, places and conversations. While salvation is always the work of God, since only God can give the gift of new life, the experience of receiving this is often unpredictable, bumpy and slow. This means that evangelism will require patience, commitment and perseverance.

Conversion as a process

Dr Lewis Rambo is a professor of psychology who has studied the concept of conversion and concluded that there are ordinarily seven different stages to a person's conversion. These seven different stages follow quite a different pattern from the experience that we see Paul undergoing on the road to Damascus and what we often hold up as a 'model' conversion testimony.[1] Rambo suggests that the *context* of conversion is often *initiated by a crisis*, which leads to *a quest* in which *encounter* and *interaction with an advocate* are important, leading to *commitment* and, lastly, *consequences*. In my experience of seeing people come to faith a more gradual process involving different stages has been more common than the dramatic conversion.

However, this can present a problem for us when some of our approaches to evangelism are based upon the assumption that people's route to faith will be more Damascus than Emmaus. This is particularly the case within my own tradition of Evangelicalism, where assumptions about the ways in which people come to faith are shaped around rousing evangelistic preaching, an opportunity to respond (often by getting up and out of your seat) and praying 'the sinner's prayer'. Within the UK, this approach finds its origin in the Wesleyan revival of the eighteenth century when John Wesley journeyed up and down the country on horseback preaching the gospel of repentance and faith, in fields and public buildings. The idea of coming forward in response to a rousing sermon became the dominant approach in churches of this tradition, encouraged further through the ministry of dynamic US preachers such as Charles Finney and D. L. Moody, who perfected the altar call. This 'crisis' model led to the assumption in many Evangelical churches that the primary way in which people become Christians is through persuasive preaching and a physical response.

The power of the altar call

The notion of the altar call continued to influence expectations of evangelism in the twentieth century, not least through Billy Graham, whose remarkable and prolific evangelistic ministry endured for over 60 years. The numerical success of his rallies affirmed Evangelical predilection for this type of evangelism, not least in Mission England, in which Graham preached to more than a million people at packed football stadiums.

I attended a gathering at Villa Park in 1984, with Sir Cliff performing and Billy Graham preaching. I recall being stirred by his preaching of the gospel and going forward on to Villa's pitch to give my life to Christ, one of many times in my youth that I did this just to make sure! At the same time I also, coincidentally, gave my life to following Aston Villa, which has proved to be a far less reliable decision!

However, over the last 30 years there has been a shift in emphasis away from this approach, for a number of reasons. We have come to see the importance of the context in which the gospel message is spoken, recognizing that it is very hard for one talk to relate to the different situations in which people find themselves. We have also had to do some serious soul searching about the significant drop-off rates that followed such mass evangelistic events.

In its place, enquirers' courses have become more important, with the gentle approach of Alpha, Christianity Explored or Pilgrim providing a more gradual exploration of the Christian faith. Church-planting has become higher on the agenda through the recognition that the witness of a Christian community is more powerful than a one-off event. Fresh expressions and missional communities have sought to reach out to people in contexts where they are already building relationships, in the hope of engaging with those unlikely to connect with mainstream churches. Such approaches have enabled the tailoring to context that mass evangelism could not easily do.

The move from understanding evangelism as focused on one definitive event to a longer process is also talked about as a reversal of the process of believing and then belonging. In today's world, belonging can often be the starting point for people rather than the destination.

Preaching the gospel

Such considerations about the changing context for evangelism raise an important question about the role of evangelistic preaching. There is a danger that we throw the proverbial baby out with the bathwater and assume that, because people in our culture today no longer turn out in their droves to hear an evangelist preaching, this model is entirely redundant. In Acts we see the importance of evangelistic preaching of the gospel. The Apostle Paul makes a point of public preaching in the major cities he visits, despite the often mixed reception. We must continue to find creative ways to preach the gospel of Jesus in public places. It is a good idea to hold guest services as part of our regular pattern of services, where congregation members can invite people to hear the gospel. It is often the case that even when the journey towards faith can take a long time for people, a stirring call to response can be a significant milestone along the way. We must also avoid the temptation to allow the criticism of a particular model of evangelism to become an excuse for doing nothing. Moody once famously said, when faced with criticism for his style of preaching, that while he too didn't care much for this form of evangelism, 'on balance, I prefer my way of doing it than your way of not doing it'. We need regular opportunities to invite friends to church services where the gospel is powerfully and relevantly preached with guests in mind. The results might be rather surprising.

At university, I had the privilege of getting to know the Revd Dr Michael Green, who preached at the university-wide mission to which I invited my housemate Chris. I don't think in all my life I have ever met another person who oozed so much infectious joy for Jesus and took every opportunity to tell people about Jesus, with a glint in his eye and a beaming smile across his face. When he died in February 2019 at the age of 88, his friends and family reported that right until the very end he continued to witness to staff and patients from his hospital bed, full of the joy and hope that had characterized his life.

Michael was someone who spent his entire life preaching the gospel and providing opportunities for people to respond to the compelling love of God in Jesus. I got married the year after leaving university and Michael kindly agreed to preach at our wedding. I knew that in his characteristically winsome way he would make the most of a church packed full of guests, many of whom did not usually darken the doors of a church. After speaking to us as a couple and extolling the virtues of marriage with Christ at the centre, he then turned to the congregation to speak of the extravagant love of God for them also. His closing words took us somewhat by surprise: 'And if one of you here today wanted to give your life to Jesus that would be the cherry on the top of Gavin and Hannah's wedding cake!' Thankfully he didn't offer an actual altar call but I do know of at least one person who went up to him at the end of the service and took one of his 'Come Follow Me' booklets, and that moment was the catalyst for her and her whole family coming to faith. There will always be a place for evangelistic preaching and invitation. However, to put all our eggs in that one basket would lack the imagination that evangelism in our contemporary situation requires.

Faith as a journey

The reality is that for many people the journey to faith is a longer and more complicated affair than we imagine. This means that our approach also needs to adapt, becoming more imaginative to engage with those who have further to travel. I recall once asking on the final evening of a course for enquirers how people felt they had changed during the eight-week period. One man in his sixties replied that while he didn't think he had changed much in his thinking during the eight weeks, compared to where he was a year ago it was unrecognizable. For people not brought up with any sense of Christian faith, unfamiliar with the concepts of the gospel, schooled in the individualism and consumerism so endemic in our society, progress can sometimes seem slow. Shifting our thinking away from the need to create the environment for a crisis point, and instead thinking in terms of a journey can really help. For those of us who were brought up in a Christian family, it can be hard to realize just how big a shift it is for people to believe in the Christian gospel. Concepts that simply make sense to us can seem completely nonsensical to others. It can all take time and we must not allow ourselves to grow impatient or get too easily discouraged.

Our role as witness is often more akin to nudging people along the pathway than to running and completing a sprint. Such nudging evangelism requires patience, perseverance and all the creative skills at our disposal. We may meet someone who has barely started on their faith journey and our role is to spark interest in the Christian faith. We may meet someone who has been thinking about the Christian faith for a while and our role might be to patiently and seriously help them work through some of the questions they have. Thinking in terms of steps along a pathway can free us from the burden of feeling we have to bring someone to a moment of commitment straight away. It can be more helpful to ask ourselves the question, 'What is the next step this person needs to make on their faith journey?' What is the most appropriate thing you could say to a work colleague to help that person on the journey to faith? What might be the next step for the friend you have just met? All of these approaches are beautiful evangelism in practice, responding intelligently and individually to the person before us.

As you travel through Lent it might be interesting to reflect upon your own faith journey and some of the key moments and influences along the way. This exercise can often help us be more understanding about other people's journey to faith. Here are some of the steps that I have found people often need to make, which have helped me value the stages along the way and not just the moment of commitment.

Establishing trust

A starting point on someone's faith journey can simply be moving forward from their negative preconception of the Christian faith. There are all kinds of assumptions that people have about what the Church or Christians are like, assumptions too often sadly stemming from people's own experiences. One does not have to look far in the pages of the newspaper to see genuine reasons why people have a negative impression of the Church, and for that we must be humble and never defensive. Television often does not help us here. Vicars on TV are either a source of comedy for being loveable but ultimately ineffectual, in the case of the Vicar of Dibley or the Revd Adam Smallbone from *Rev*, or else they are inwardly conflicted, as in the case of the 'hot priest' from *Fleabag*. In my opinion, only Sean Bean's portrayal of a Catholic priest in the BBC drama *Broken* goes near an authentic portrayal. Thankfully Radio 4's *Three Vicars Talking* allowed clergy to speak for themselves and dispel some of the unhelpful myths.[2]

When we meet someone and talk to them about Christianity the chances are they already have an idea in their head of what the Church is all about and it may well be a reason why they have already discounted it as being relevant to their lives. A starting point can be as simple as building trust and helping people to have a different, and hopefully improved, picture of what a Christian is. People have some inkling that Christians are supposed to be loving and kind, but when that is not reinforced through their actual experience, the sense of disconnect sets in. Evangelism flourishes best in and through friendships, and in such relationships the integrity of Christian discipleship is paramount.

Once I was on a train from London to Cardiff. The train was packed and so I found myself standing in the section between the two carriages. I got into conversation with someone who was also unable to find a seat and we talked about our jobs. I was working in student ministry at the time and he told me that he was a fraud investigator. We chatted for a while and then I noticed that the ticket inspector was starting to make his way down the length of the carriage towards us. I bent down to get my ticket out of my bag and noticed my new 'friend' dive into the toilet. As he closed the door he put his finger to his lips. It took me a few moments to register what was happening, but once I realized he was travelling without a ticket all respect I had for him as a fraud investigator went right out of the window.

Integrity is a synthesis between words and action. Witnessing is about living out the story of Jesus as well as speaking it. We are often the embodiment of the message to people before we get the opportunity to speak. Beautiful evangelism can never just be about clever words that we say. One of the first nudges along the way can be the simple step of establishing trust. Something that friends used to say to me was, 'If you ran a church I might consider going . . .' (I think they might have slightly regretted those words once I got ordained!) However, I don't think they were saying that I would be better than other people at leading churches, but they were acknowledging that the gap between what they think the Church is (their negative preconception) and the reality is slowly being bridged. Trust had been formed. A step had been taken along the journey towards faith.

Sparking interest

If people do not have a negative impression of the Church then the chances are they think it is largely irrelevant to their lives. As Christians we need to become better at arousing curiosity about the Christian faith. Yet somehow, despite the fact that we have the most interesting subject matter possible, we have managed to give the impression that the Christian faith is dull and boring. So how do we become better at arousing curiosity in others? The key is in saying less than we think. As we have already seen, Jesus is the master of the perfectly phrased question, the one comment that lingers in the air long after it has left his lips. Our tendency to think we have to say everything means that we leave people feeling over full rather than wanting more. Far better to drop one slightly provocative question or comment into the conversation than preach at someone for ten minutes. We need to see our conversations sometimes more like appetisers than a huge Christmas dinner.

Imagine you are at work on Monday morning and someone asks you how your weekend was. You could narrate a list of things you had done, throwing in that you went to church, or you could say, 'Well, church was pretty incredible this week', or, 'I was struck by something that was said at church.' These kinds of statements are more likely to open up the question 'What happened?' or 'Tell me more'. Developing the habit of throwing in curiosity-arousing comments about your life as a follower of Jesus can make people wonder whether Christianity might be more interesting than they had assumed. Evangelism needs to be imaginative, using the skills and gifts that we have to arouse interest and intrigue. Those in our churches who have creative gifts in music, poetry and art can have something really precious to contribute to the evangelistic ministry of the Church.

My sister Bekah runs a toddlers' music group called 'Music Makers' in her church in North Devon. Each week parents and carers attend with their children, enjoying the music and creative stories from the Bible using puppets and crafts. Many of these families never attend church on a Sunday. During the lockdown my sister took to recording a few songs and a story each week, which she put online where they were watched by over a hundred families. One dad in particular didn't normally attend the group but working from home meant that he was able to watch with his 4-year-old daughter for the first time. His daughter was so intrigued by the stories from the Bible that she asked her dad whether she could hear more and so he went out to buy a Bible he could read to her. Though he hadn't attended church since he was a child, as he read these stories and watched online he too found himself drawn to Jesus and eventually decided he wanted to follow him.

Developing an open mind

An important stage in the journey for people can be moving from a place of thinking that Christianity is interesting to thinking that it might have something to say to them. This can be a common stage at which people get stuck, enjoying debating and discussing ideas without being open to change. It is during this period that sharing our story is most effective. Since people today are often less concerned with the objective truth of Christianity and more interested in whether it works in practice, conversations about the difference Christianity makes in our lives can be really helpful. As we have seen, it is not necessarily about the dramatic, life-changing testimonies but simply speaking of the continuing reality of Jesus in our day-to-day lives, the small answers to prayer, and the strength and help through difficult times.

This stage of growing openness can be slow. It is not easy to change our worldview. People's mindsets are often quite fixed and it takes a lot of imagination to consider that the world might be different from how you imagined. It is important that we recognize this and are prepared to journey alongside people where possible.

When we first moved into our house a local plumber came to sort out some problems in our bathroom. Mike was really friendly and I could tell from the things that he listened to on the radio as he worked that he enjoyed thinking about deep questions, and we soon struck up a conversation about Christianity. Mike was an ardent atheist but he enjoyed debating with me. I don't think he had met a Christian before who was willing to talk about their reasons for faith. Mike spent a couple of weeks at our house and we enjoyed lots of conversations over this period of time. When he left I gave him a copy of Tim Keller's *The Reason for God* because I thought this would help him think further about the things we had talked about.[3] He was grateful and said he would read it, but I didn't see him again for a long time.

Four years later we needed some work doing on our heating and so I got in touch with Mike to see if he was still working in the area, and whether he could come and help us out. He turned up at my house the next day and the first thing he said to me was, 'I read that book you gave me.' 'Oh, I'm glad,' I replied. 'What did you think of it?' 'Well,' he said, with a smile on his face, 'I'm no longer an atheist. Now I'm an agnostic!' Slow progress I thought, but we are heading in a good direction. We continued to talk further over the course of the next week and I did notice a different openness. I tried to suggest to him that if he thought God could possibly exist then why didn't he try praying? Mike was pretty sceptical about this and didn't think it was a good idea at all. He was now content that the idea of God was a possibility but he didn't think there was any way he could know for certain and so was happy to leave it at that. He also told me that he was moving out of London, so I knew it was unlikely I would see him again.

Six years later I was working from home one day when the doorbell rang. Opening it, I was surprised to see Mike on the doorstep. He said that he happened to be in the area for the day and thought he would see if I was in. I invited him in for a cup of tea and we got chatting. He told me that the day before had been the burial of his mother. It was a church funeral as his mother was a Christian, something he had not previously mentioned in our conversations. We had a good and really honest chat about life, death and faith. This time when he left I urged him once again to try praying. As he said farewell and headed off down the path, his final words were, 'Do you know, I might just give it a try this time.'

The journey towards faith will be long and circuitous for many in our culture today, with twists and turns along the way. Sometimes we do not get to see the whole picture; we might instead be a link in the chain, a nudge along the pathway. Our role as witnesses is to be present where we can, to discern what God might be saying to us to help that person take the next step along the path and to trust God in the in-between times still to be at work. Our role is not to give up.

Asking questions

Once someone is open to exploring the Christian faith then they tend to have a lot of questions. At this stage an enquirers' course like Christianity Explored, Talking Pictures or Alpha can be really useful. Creating safe spaces where people can ask questions and air their opinions is often a hugely important step along the way. If, like me, you have been a Christian all of your life or have at least been familiar with church, then it is sometimes hard to grasp just how big a leap it is for people. We need to create hospitable communities where people can explore, ask questions and know that no question is too silly or obvious, difficult or controversial. I often find that people think that I am going to be offended by their questions or lack of faith, so it's crucial to create the kind of environment where people can speak candidly and freely.

Affirming people's questions and the importance of them can be vital: we need to take them seriously. It's a privilege when people ask questions and want to engage with Christianity and so we should respect their opinions and the objections they might make. Sometimes such questions genuinely express the things that hold people back from faith; we need to deal with them wisely and graciously. I used to think that I was only being an effective witness if I could answer every question, but I have come to see that I don't need to have all the answers. It's okay to say to someone, 'I've never thought about that before. Do you mind if I think about that and come back to you on another day?' People will respect you more if you do that rather than try to answer a question you don't feel equipped for. How we answer people can speak more powerfully than what we actually have to say. It's possible to win the argument but lose the person. Peter reminds us that we are to answer people's questions with 'gentleness and reverence' (1 Peter 3.15), giving attention to our attitude and heart as much as our words.

It can be a great stage in someone's journey in which to suggest reading the Bible, either individually or together. I often encourage a person to start with Mark's Gospel because it is simple and short. You don't need to be a skilled Bible study leader to do this. Meeting together and reading a small section of the Bible and asking some simple questions isn't as complicated as you think.

Growing up in a vicarage meant that I was used to people coming and going for all sorts of meetings. One regular guest in my teenage years was a man in his eighties named Eric, who unexpectedly turned up to church one morning. He had recently been bereaved and was feeling lonely, which was made worse by tensions and broken relationships within his family. A friend had suggested he tried church, although Eric had not attended since the age of 16. My dad invited him to the vicarage that week and they started studying the Bible together. Eric was keen to learn and explore more about the Bible, and used to turn up to the sessions with mini essays he had written in advance. My dad had not anticipated this, but Eric lapped it all up, hungry to hear and learn. Over time, Eric came to know the transforming love of Jesus and his life took on a new purpose and direction. He spent his remaining years serving in the church and seeking to build the broken relationships within his family. When he died he left his box of books to the church, books that he had purchased during his years of faith. I still have one of his books on discipleship; every sentence is underlined. It was as if he was trying to absorb as much as he could in the time that he had left. The love of Jesus had totally transformed his life.

Following Jesus

Our hope and prayer as we engage with people through these different stages of the journey is that there will come a point when they want to follow Jesus. Similar to the parable of the hidden treasure that we looked at in chapter 1, Jesus also told the parable of the pearl of great price (Matthew 13.45–46). In this story the merchant sells all that he has to buy one pearl that is of greater value than any other. What Jesus is looking for is not people who are pearl-connoisseurs, or those who study and understand the value of pearls, but people who will sell all they have to hold this one pearl. Jesus is not looking for admirers but followers. It can feel scary to ask the question, 'Would you like to follow Jesus?', but there is no question more important in the world. It is vital that we regularly and naturally make that kind of invitation as part of our normal church services. There are those whom God brings along in an unexpected way, who need to hear that invitation. There are also those who have sat in our pews for weeks on end but aren't really sure if their faith is personal to them. It should be the most natural invitation in the world to make.

I once led a daytime Alpha course with a group of new mums. One of the women in church had invited her antenatal group to do Alpha and almost all of them agreed to come along. We met for a few weeks, watching the talks and discussing while the babies crawled around and created happy chaos. On the evening we had set aside to talk about the Holy Spirit, only two mums turned up and I secretly felt a little disappointed. We enjoyed a meal together, and after a short talk on the Holy Spirit I knew it was time to offer to pray for the two mums. I didn't want them to feel awkward and so I mumbled something fairly generic, along the lines, 'Is there anything you would like me to pray for? It can be anything at all.' There was an awkward silence as both of the women looked to the ground. Then one of them looked up and said tentatively, 'I was wondering if it was possible to ask Jesus into my life?' I nearly fell off my chair – this was not what I had expected! Concerned by how the other woman might be reacting, I glanced over at her and she caught my eye and then muttered, 'If it's okay with you, I would like to do the same.' This was one of the most joyous and precious moments of my life, leading these two women in a simple prayer inviting Jesus into their lives. Many tears were shed that night as these two women encountered for the first time the pearl of great price, holding it in their hands and marvelling at its beauty.

Reflecting on this story later I was grateful that while the boldness of their question had taken me by surprise, the response had not, and I was glad that in that moment I knew what to say. Someone recently asked me, 'What's the process of becoming a Christian? What do I have to do?' He was surprised by my answer, 'Oh, it's very simple really, you just have to say yes to Jesus.' As we have seen, evangelism is taking people to Jesus, just as Philip did with Nathanael. The Bible uses the language of receiving Christ (John 1.12), believing in Christ (John 3.16) and entering into the kingdom (John 3.5) to describe the process of becoming a Christian. While new life in Christ is a gift from God, it is still something we have to receive or, more simply, say yes to. One of the passages most appropriate is Revelation 3.20:

Listen! I am standing at the door, knocking; if you hear my voice and open the door, I will come in to you and eat with you, and you with me.

This is such a powerful image for someone on the verge of becoming a Christian – they are hearing the gentle knock of Jesus on the door of their heart. There is a wonderful video of Pope Francis speaking on this passage to a crowd in South America in 2015. He describes this verse with the Spanish phrase 'toca timbre', meaning 'ring the doorbell'. Jesus is ringing the doorbell of our hearts. All we have to do is open the door and invite him in, and he will come and feast with us. This simple prayer isn't an invitation to a one-off experience or event but is an invitation to a continuing journey with Jesus as he comes to live in us.

That night on the Alpha course, leading those two women in prayer didn't require fancy words or lengthy explanations. I merely said a simple prayer that they could echo in their own hearts:

Lord Jesus,
I am sorry that I have been living life my own way.
Thank you that you died for me and rose from the dead.
Please come into my life by your Spirit and be with me for ever.
Amen.

These aren't magic words. There is no secret formula to entry into the kingdom other than repentance and faith, which can be expressed in a myriad ways. Our role as witnesses is to be prepared so that when the opportunity comes we know what to say. Helping someone to say yes to Jesus is one of the greatest privileges that life can hold. How beautiful are the feet of those who bring good news.

Helping others to live his story

The goal of our witness, however, isn't simply getting people to 'pray the prayer' so we can move on to the next person. Jesus didn't commission his disciples to make converts but to make disciples: 'baptizing them . . . and teaching them to obey everything that I have commanded you' (Matthew 28.19–20). As we saw in Chapter 1, evangelism is an invitation to find our place in God's story. The good news of Jesus is not just about believing but receiving life in Jesus' name. The goal of our witness is to initiate people into life in the kingdom of God. Imaginative evangelism cannot simply be opening the door to people and then leaving them to figure it out on their own. The first few weeks and months as a follower of Jesus are critical. Discipleship does not happen overnight. There are some things that will come naturally but others that will need to be learned and taught.

One of these is helping new believers get started on the Bible if they haven't read it before. We can't assume people will know how to do this. It is a hugely daunting book with over a thousand pages; where should you begin? I always suggest that people start with a Gospel (Luke or Mark) and then Genesis, followed by John, Exodus and Romans. It can be good to introduce people early to the Psalms and perhaps encourage them to read one a day as they pray. There are lots of great guides available and the Bible App in particular has some great reading outlines, but you might need to help new believers so they don't feel overwhelmed. Ideally you would meet with them to read the Bible or suggest that they join a small group in the church to discuss with other Christians.

Teaching a new believer to pray is also something we might take for granted if we have been a Christian for a while. But prayer can seem intimidating to those who are new, especially praying out loud if that is your church's normal practice. A friend once told me about a woman who had just become a Christian and was nervous about praying out loud. My friend reassured this rather well-to-do woman that all she had to do was talk to God as she would any other person and he would hear her. There was a silence as the woman bowed her head, cleared her throat and then said in a very loud voice, 'Good evening, God'. Those who are unfamiliar with church might need help in understanding why we do and say certain things. Why do we stand up at certain points? Why do we bow our heads or wave our arms? Whatever our church tradition, there will be things that are unfamiliar and might need some explaining.

However, in many ways, some of these issues of Bible study, prayer and church are relatively simple; discipleship itself is more complicated. While an entire book could be written on discipleship alone, let's consider three things that might help people in the early stages of Christian faith.

Discipleship takes time

Tertullian, a third-century apologist for the faith in North Africa, said this about discipleship: 'Christians are made, not born.' Conversion might happen in an instant but discipleship happens over a lifetime. The point at which someone decides they want to follow Jesus is only the beginning of a long journey. Discipleship will not be done and dusted with an intensive course during Lent. We need to be prepared to travel and journey with people over a long period of time. When someone becomes a Christian today they are already a disciple, just a disciple of other things, whether that is the culture of consumerism or individualism. Because we are so used to being in charge of our own future and destiny, surrendering control to God can be a slow process of learning.

We need to explore creative ways to engage people in long-term discipleship, as quick fixes often do not last long. We may fear that people are put off by anything that seems intensive or too heavy, but new habits and patterns do not form overnight. People devote endless hours to developing routines of physical fitness and healthy eating, knowing that those lifestyle changes do not happen instantly. The same is true with discipleship. Yes, the Spirit can work in miraculous ways and people are sometimes set free from addictions or other internal battles at the point of conversion, but for many the road of discipleship is more complicated and bumpy. People's lives are complex and messy, and if we are going to be committed to journey with people in discipleship then we will need patience, love and perseverance, and we will need to make this a priority in the life of our church.

My friend Will became a Christian in prison. As a teenager he had got in with the wrong crowd, started taking drugs, and at the age of 19 found himself facing criminal charges for assault, after which he spent a year in prison. In prison he encountered Christ in a miraculous way, and when he was released from prison he started attending the local church. He soon found that his old life started catching up with him; old dealers re-established contact and he found it hard to break the cycle. He got to know a couple in the church who invited him to come and live with them. Will told me that every time he was tempted to go and connect with his old life, the couple would lead him into the kitchen, put the kettle on and sit down with him for a cup of tea. He said that their patience and love for him over that first crucial year was the turning point in his life, although he said he had never drunk so much tea before. Their persistence and generosity helped him through that bumpy first year of discipleship and provided him with a foundation from which he could then build the rest of his life, which later included working full time in his local church.

Discipleship takes place in community

One of the devastating impacts of individualism on the Church is that we have made conversion into a purely personal affair, as if it is only about 'me and my faith'. When the first disciples followed Jesus they had a personal encounter with Christ, but they also became part of a community. In describing the transformation that takes place when we encounter Jesus, the Apostle Peter wrote this in his first letter:

> But you are a chosen race, a royal priesthood, a holy nation, God's own people, in order that you may proclaim the mighty acts of him who called you out of darkness into his marvellous light.

> Once you were not a people,
>   but now you are God's people;
> once you had not received mercy,
>   but now you have received mercy.
> (1 Peter 2.9–10)

To become a disciple is to become part of God's family, the community that he is building to be a blessing to the world. Discipleship is not a personal affair, it is corporate. We need to ask ourselves whether our churches are welcoming places where new Christians can find a home. Do we have time and space to build the kind of relationships that people need to help them truly feel part of a community?

The word 'disciple' is used over 200 times in the book of Acts but the disciples are rarely alone. When Jesus is transfigured he takes Peter, James and John with him. When Jesus sends his disciples out to preach the gospel he sends them in twos. Jesus is repeatedly seen gathering his disciples around him for meals and for teaching. When the Holy Spirit falls upon the disciples, Luke tells us, 'they were all together in one place' (Acts 2.1). Discipleship has always been about community and it is in the community of faith that the seeds of the gospel start to take root, bear fruit and in time produce yet more seeds.

Discipleship means getting involved

One of the legacies of our Western Enlightenment understanding of reality is that we tend to think of the life of faith in terms of 'believing and understanding the right things'. However, when you read the book of Acts, the emphasis seems also to be on the way the first disciples live. In Acts 2 we learn that the disciples met together for teaching and fellowship, but we also read of the impact they had on those around them, serving the poor, ensuring the widows and orphans were provided for. Discipleship is about believing, but it is also about rolling up your sleeves and getting stuck in with the life of the kingdom.

As a parent of teenage sons, the gaming console can be a source of family tension. One day my son seemed to be playing on it for a particularly long time and I was trying to encourage him to join the rest of us for a family film. I asked him what it was about gaming that was so enthralling. His response really struck me. 'The thing is,' he said, 'with a movie, someone else has already decided what will happen and how it will end; with a computer game, I get to create the future. I get to decide what happens.'

When we present Christian discipleship as a list of things to believe and know, we misunderstand its true nature. The invitation to follow Jesus is an invitation to a life of adventure. It is an invitation to get involved, to make a difference. Our words and actions make a difference. Discipleship is not just about believing the facts of the gospel story, but living it. We get to live in the kingdom, to pursue justice, care for creation, serve with compassion and speak the good news of the one who has risen from the dead. For many, this journey may be long and complicated and will require all the creativity and perseverance we can muster. However, as we have seen, it is ultimately the miraculous work of the Spirit to bring new life, and our role as witness is more often that of a gentle nudge along the pathway as we journey with people. As we pass on this good news to others they too, in time, join in adding their words and their actions to the testimony of 2,000 years of witnesses who proclaim the simple truth, 'I have seen.'

For discussion

1 This Lent, reflect upon your own faith journey and ask yourself: What are the key moments that stand out? Who has influenced and helped you?

2 How do you feel the story of your journey to faith affects others? How do those of others affect you?

3 What are some of the ways you might be able to help gently nudge people along the pathway to faith?

Conclusion

The gospel of Jesus Christ is the most remarkable story we will ever hear. It is a story of redemption, sacrifice and love, with the power to transform lives. The gospel narrative stands at the centre of Holy Week as we turn our hearts towards a bloodied Saviour on the cross, who would spend himself in love for sinners like you and me. As we prepare for the celebration of Easter we remember a cosmic turning point in human history, when death is defeated and new life is made possible in Christ.

On that first Easter morning, God could have chosen to make the news of Jesus' miraculous resurrection known in any number of ways. He could have emblazoned a declaration across the sky so all could have seen it and not doubted its veracity. He could have had Jesus appear alive in the presence of the crowd who had bayed for his death. However, God chose the lips of ordinary women, whose hearts were broken with grief, now erupting with joy, to be the vessels through which he would pass on this life-changing news. God chose ordinary people, with personal stories of redemption and imperfect words, to tell the greatest news there has ever been.

God continues to use people like you and me to share the life-changing news of the gospel of Jesus. We are the ordinary people through whom God is bringing about a revolution of his extraordinary love. The mandate remains the same but the context is different. There is no guarantee that our experience of witness will be easy; we should certainly not underestimate the challenges that lie before us. Our task is to engage in evangelism that is both beautiful and imaginative. We are to bear witness in such a way that speaks to people's hearts and minds, connecting their stories with God's great story, so that in Christ they might find new life and meaning. Let us hear his voice this Holy Week calling to us as it did to Mary that first Easter morning: 'Go and tell'. As we seek to live the story of the gospel we are privileged to reveal his extra-ordinary love in ordinary ways, putting our name to his story and inviting others to join us as we do so. There is no task more urgent or wonderful than this.

Notes

Introduction

1 William J. Abraham, *The Logic of Evangelism,* London: Hodder & Stoughton, 1989, p. 202.

1 The greatest story of all time

1 Robert McKee, *Story: Substance, Structure, Style and Principles of Screenwriting,* New York: HarperCollins, 1997.

2 Walter Brueggemann, *Biblical Perspectives on Evangelism: Living in a Three-storied Universe,* Nashville, TN: Abingdon Press, 1993, p. 11.

3 <www.barna.com/research/millennials-oppose-evangelism/> (accessed 17 June 2020).

4 <www.theguardian.com/world/2018/sep/07/church-in-crisis-as-only-2-of-young-adults-identify-as-c-of-e> (accessed 8 September 2018).

5 Stanley Hauerwas, *Approaching the End: Eschatological Reflection on Church, Politics and Life,* Grand Rapids, MI: Eerdmans, 2013, p. 51.

6 Rebecca Manley Pippert, *Out of the Saltshaker and into the World: Evangelism as a Way of Life,* Leicester: IVP, 1999, p. 11.

7 John Finney, *Finding Faith Today: How Does It Happen?,* Swindon: Bible Society, 1992, p. 46.

8 J. John, *Breaking News: A Practical Course Designed to Help You Share God's Good News,* Bletchley: Authentic Media, 2006, p. 41.

9 From a lecture delivered at St Mellitus College, London, 2016.

10 Gail Honeyman, *Eleanor Oliphant is Completely Fine,* London: HarperCollins, 2018.

11 *Dr Strange,* US: Marvel Studios, 2016.

12 Willie Jennings, *Acts (Belief: a Theological Commentary on the Bible),* Louisville, KY: Westminster John Knox Press, 2017, p. 178.

13 P. Weston, *Lesslie Newbigin: Missionary Theologian: A Reader*, London: SPCK, 2006, p. 250.

2 Catching up with God

1 David Wenham, *The Parables of Jesus*, Downers Grove, ILL: InterVarsity Press, 1989, p. 225.
2 Pope Francis, *The Joy of the Gospel: Evangelii Gaudium*, USCCB, 2013, p. 125.
3 <https://archive.org/stream/HudsonTaylor-InEarlyYears-TheGrowth OfASoul-1911Printed-Brought/HudsonTaylor-InEarlyYears-The GrowthOfASoul#page/n217/mode/2up> (accessed 10 March 2020).
4 David Watson, *I Believe in Evangelism*, London: Hodder & Stoughton, 1976.

3 Jesus was in the transformation business

1 Rowan Williams, *Resurrection: Interpreting the Easter Gospel*, London: Darton, Longman & Todd, 2002, p. 61.
2 Bryan Stone, *Evangelism after Pluralism: The Ethics of Christian Witness*, Grand Rapids, MI: Baker Academic, 2018, p. 9.

4 Communicating like Jesus did

1 Thomas Erikson, *Surrounded by Idiots: The Four Types of Human Behavior and How to Effectively Communicate with Each in Business (and in Life)*, New York: Macmillan, 2019.
2 G. Noort, K. Avtzi and S. Paas eds, *Sharing Good News: Handbook on Evangelism in Europe*, Geneva: WCC Publications, 2017, p. 283.
3 <https://talkingjesus.org/research-from-the-course/> (accessed 24 June 2020).
4 Pete Ward, *Youth Culture and the Gospel*, Basingstoke: Marshall Pickering, 1992.
5 David Male and Paul Weston, *The Word's Out: Speaking the Gospel Today*, Abingdon: BRF, 2013.

5 Passing on the story of Jesus

1 John V. Taylor, *The Go-Between God: The Holy Spirit and the Christian Mission*, London: SCM Press, 1975, p. 53.

2 Tom Wright, *God and the Pandemic: A Christian Reflection on the Coronavirus and its Aftermath*, London: SPCK, 2020.

3 Mark Ireland and Mike Booker, *Making New Disciples: Exploring the Paradoxes of Evangelism*, London: SPCK, 2015, p. 69.

4 *Call the Midwife Christmas Special*, UK: BBC, 2019.

5 Rodney Stark, *The Rise of Christianity: A Sociologist Reconsiders History*, Princeton, NJ: Princeton University Press, 1996.

6 Finding echoes of the story of Jesus in our world today

1 Steve Hollinghurst, *Mission Shaped Evangelism: The Gospel in Contemporary Culture*, Norwich: Canterbury Press, 2010, p. 168.

2 <www.independent.co.uk/news/media/tv-radio/average-watching-tv-briton-10-years-life-research-a8367526.html> (accessed 15 July 2020).

3 <https://advanced-television.com/2020/04/24/research-lockdowns-profound-effect-on-uk-tv-viewing/> (accessed 15 July 2020).

4 Alister E. McGrath, *Mere Apologetics*, London: SPCK, 2016, p. 96.

5 Jordan Peterson, *12 Rules for Life: An Antidote to Chaos*, London: Penguin, 2018.

6 <www.youtube.com/watch?v=dzkspSXg2tM#action=share> (accessed 8 July 2020).

7 Brian Christian, *The Most Human Human: What Artificial Intelligence Teaches Us about Being Alive*, London: Penguin, 2012.

8 Ian McEwan *Machines Like Me*, London: Penguin, 2019.

7 Stories of finding Jesus

1 Lewis Rambo, *Understanding Religious Conversion*, New Haven, CT: Yale University Press, 1993.

2 The series can now be read as a book: Richard Coles, Kate Bottley, Giles Fraser, *Three Vicars Talking*, London: SPCK, 2020.

3 Timothy Keller, *The Reason for God: Belief in an Age of Scepticism*, London: Hodder & Stoughton, 2008.